PAIN, PROMISCUITY, PURPOSE

PAIN, PROMISCUITY, PURPOSE

FROM MESS TO MINISTRY

KENDRA FOWLER

Ministry in Writing

Washington, D.C.

Published by: Ministry in Writing Publishing Company, Washington D.C.

ISBN: 978-0-692-92084-8

Resources:

Scripture quotations marked KJV are taken from the Holy Bible, King James Version, 1611

Scripture quotations marked (NLT) are taken from the Holy Bible, New Living Translation, copyright © 1996, 2004, 2007 by Tyndale House Foundation. Used by permission of Tyndale House Publishers, Inc., Carol Stream, Illinois 60188. All rights reserved.

www.prevention.com. Philip Goldberg, 02 Dec. 2011. Web. <http://www.prevention.com/mind-body/emotional-health/recover-unhappy-childhood>.

Cover and book design by Tyora Moody, Tywebbin Creations www.tywebbincreations.com

Editing by Donna Poole and Kimberlee Kiefer, Writing by Design thepittsfordpooles@gmail.com

Disclaimer: Some of the names and minor details in this book have been changed to protect the privacy of individuals.

Contents

Thank You

Thank You, Father, for my story. I thank You for forgiving me, growing me, using me, delivering me, transforming me, protecting me, and never taking Your hands off me. I thank You for every good or bad thing that happened in my life that brought me closer to You. I thank You for causing all things to work together for my good. I thank You for all the prayers you answered and the prayers you didn't answer. Thank You for showing me favor. Sometimes I still sit and wonder, why me? I did not and do not deserve the love and grace You've shown me. I am a sinner, yet you love me. I have broken pieces and you love me. I have turned my back on You many times. Still, You love me. I thank You for being a God of second chances. I thank for being my strength. I thank You for being my Jehovah Rapha, my Jehovah Jireh, and my Jehovah Shalom. I thank You for the moment you made it so I had no choice but to call on You. You are El Shaddai and all my praise belong to You. For without You, I am nothing. It is for your glory that I share my story so others may know of Your healing power and transforming power.

Kyelia, Kyelia, Kyelia. Mommy's favorite girl. I remember telling you one day that I didn't know if I could finish this book and you said, "Don't say that. Yes you can!" That was just one of the many ways you encourage me. Sometimes I wonder, who is the mother here? I never knew it was possible to love this much until I had you. There is nothing I love more than you except the Creator who blessed me with you. You, my girl, are wise beyond your years, extremely talented, energetic, and funny and nothing makes me happier than hearing you call me Mommy. I vow to be the best mother I can be as long as I have breath in my body. My prayer is that you will never part from the foundation I've set for you. No matter what, I want you to always pray and stay in God's Word. The world is going to try to pull you away from it, but I pray you stand firm on what you know to be true. I love you baby girl.

Mommy I miss you so much and I thank you for turning your life around just in time to give me the most loving childhood a child could ask for. I knew without a doubt that you loved me more than anything in the world. You did the best you could and I'm grateful for the 10 years I had with you. I will love you forever.

Aunt Tricia, I remember you used to say, "You're gonna miss me when I'm gone." And boy do I? If I could have one wish, it would be to rewind back to our last conversation. I would've stay longer, hugged you tighter, and listened when you told me to stay a few more minutes. You were my EVERYTHING. If I tried to put into words everything you mean to me, I would be writing all day. I love you so much and will miss you forever.

Daddy, I love you. And I understand now that you loved me the way you knew how.

Paula, I will forever be grateful for how you took me in as one of your own. Without hesitation, you were there for me when you didn't have to be. Every special moment– when I got my cycle for the first time, my graduations, proms, and the birth of Kyelia– you were there. I love you so much and I thank you for coming in and being my "breath of fresh air". I'm grateful for my sisters as watching them inspired me to go after my career, open my business, and to go hard for whatever I want.

To my cousins who are more like sisters Shantay and Taijwana, Kyelia's other mommies. I appreciate and love you both so much for loving her and always there being for me. It's been hard raising her on my own but the way you both step in makes life so much easier.

To my Best Friends Forever, Amber and Toya. From running the halls of Roper Middle School to running businesses and households, I thank you for 20 years of friendship. So many people grow apart from their childhood friends and go their separate ways, but we've managed to stand the test of time. Every time we get together, we turn into the same 12 and 13 year old girls that we were years ago. I've lost friends over the years and I'm okay with that; but the thought of losing either of you literally makes my heart hurt. My forever friends. I love you both way more than I can put into words.

To Mayerlin, where do I start, woman of God? I have told you many times how instrumental you have been to my spiritual walk but I'm going to say it again. I have no idea what I would be doing if you hadn't come into my life. From our talks to you introducing me to the Christian programs that completely changed my outlook on God, parenting, marriage, and life in general. You started out as my coworker but have become one of my best friends and my sister. I love you and your family like you are my own. And I thank you for the biggest gift of all… for accepting the responsibility for Kyelia should something ever happen to me. And I can't forget to thank you, Susannah, for taking a chance and hiring me on the spot. If it wasn't for you, I wouldn't have the job that ultimately led to my spiritual growth spurt. I can't thank you enough.

To my friend/sister France, it's true when they say true friendship knows no time. Meeting the way we met and at the time we met was only God's doing. I had been praying for like-minded friends and being the above and beyond God that He is, He brought me the sister He knew I needed. Your words encourage me and your walk with God inspires me. I love you big sister.

To Covenant House of Washington DC: Thank you preparing me for real life. I don't know what would have happened if you didn't have a bed for me that night. I am forever committed to giving back in any way I can.

Shout out to my Sorors of Lambda Omicron Chi Christian Sorority, Inc! Queen thank you for mentoring me, and inspiring me. I praise God that you answered the call to begin this organization. To my line sister, Belita. I thank God for putting you in my life. Your faith and the way you listen to and heed to His spirit truly inspires me. I love you for being you unapologetically. To all my Sorors, JJJJJJJCCCCCCC!!!

Thank you to everyone I couldn't name individually: My friends, family, church family, coworkers, and everyone who decides to read my story. I truly do appreciate the love, support, and encouragement you all have shown me.

Finally, I would like to thank everyone who purposely hurt me in some way. It was that very hurt that made me run into the arms of my Savior time and time again. And to my naysayers, it was every time you told me I couldn't that made me want to prove I could.

Therefore if any man be in Christ, he is a new creature: old things are passed away; behold, all things are become new.
1 Corinthians 5:17

Introduction

Writing this book has been one of the hardest, most freeing, happiest, saddest, most exciting, and scariest experiences of my life. Although I've always been very open about my life, it's another thing to write it out for the world to read. It started out as an advice book for young women, but the more I wrote, the more I felt like God was telling me, "First tell them what I did for you." And then I began coming across many confirming messages encouraging me to share my story. The need arose in me to testify about the Lord's favor and His transforming power.

My prayer is that after reading this book, you will be inspired. Inspired to give your life to Christ if you haven't already. Inspired to break free from whatever has you bound. Inspired to forgive the person or persons who did the unforgivable. Inspired to answer the call you feel in your spirit. One thing you'll notice throughout my story is that I constantly felt a pulling from the Lord, but I ran from it. If you're experiencing that same feeling, I pray you embrace it rather than run away from it.

In Mark 5:19, Jesus told the man whom he had freed from demon possession to go and tell everyone what He had done for him. Have you been freed from bondage like the man? Jesus didn't free you for you to keep quiet about it. He wants you to talk about it. Has He been good to you? He wants you to talk about it. I pray that reading my story inspires you to share your own.

Chapter 1

Goodbye, Mommy

"Mommy has AIDS," my sister, Kelly, said on the other end of the telephone. "Do you understand what I'm telling you?" she asked after a few moments of silence. "Mommy is dying."

No, I didn't understand. I just wanted my sister to stop trying to make me understand. At ten years old, I didn't really know what AIDS was. I had heard of it and knew it was a disease, but I didn't know Mommy had it.

Everything was moving so fast; I didn't understand what was happening. Mommy had just been lying on the couch like she did any other day; the next thing I knew we were calling an ambulance, and now my sister was telling me she's dying. It was all too much for me. My sister kept me on the phone trying to calm me down, but I couldn't hear anything she was saying. I didn't want to hear anymore, so I gave the phone back to my Aunt Mae, who had been staying with us. Aunt Mae held me while she talked on the phone, rocking me back and forth.

I sat there thinking about everything that had happened. Earlier that evening, we had all sat around watching TV. Mommy was lying in her normal spot on the couch; Aunt Mae was sitting in a chair. I was perched at the end of the couch beside my mother's feet, which was where I always sat. This time was different; Mommy kept kicking me. I paid it no mind at first. Mommy was a very playful person, always poking and prodding to make fun, so I figured she was just playing. But, what started out as light kicks turned into hard and painful kicks.

"Ouch, Mommy! You're kicking me," I complained, rubbing my leg.

"Oh, I'm sorry." She jumped as if I startled her. She went back to watching TV but continued kicking me.

"Mommy, you're still kicking me."

This time she didn't respond. She looked around the room as if she didn't know where she was. I had never seen her act like this, and it was beginning to scare me. My brother, Damion, heard the commotion from the back room, and he came out to see what was going on.

"Mommy keeps kicking me," I told him, now in tears. He motioned for me to stand beside him. Mommy was still looking around like she was trying to figure out where she was.

"Ma, what's going on? You're scaring Peaches," he said to her. She looked down at the end of the couch where I normally sat.

"She's right here, Ma." He sounded scared himself. "She's standing right here. Look at her…she's scared."

Again, she looked at the end of the couch. We were standing directly in front of her, but it was as if she didn't see us. My brother knew something was wrong when he started asking her questions. Her response to everything he asked her was, "Peas in a pod."

Finally, he asked her, "Ma, what year is it?"

"1968." It was actually 1996.

When she said that, he called an ambulance as it was obvious she was losing her mind. The paramedics arrived, examined her, and took her to George Washington Hospital. I wasn't worried because this was the norm for her. She had been taken to the hospital by ambulance a few times before and came home after a few days. I figured this time was no different, until my sister called telling me she wasn't coming back home this time.

I couldn't believe this was happening. I'd had visions of Mommy dying, but I'd never thought it would actually happen.

In those visions, I was walking through the house knocking things down and screaming. But I didn't do any of that. I didn't know what to do. I'm not sure if it had truly hit me that Mommy was dying, or, maybe it had, but I didn't think it was going to happen so fast.

I got up the next morning, eager to get to the hospital. My Aunt Tricia, my mother's sister, came to pick us up. When we got there, I noticed we were going to a different part of the hospital from where we had visited her before. This time we were visiting Mommy in the intensive care unit (ICU). Aunt Tricia said this was where the hospital kept people who were very sick.

As we walked into her room, I heard the doctor say, "She can hear and see you guys, so she'll know you're in the room."

It still had not hit me yet, and then I walked into her room. Nothing could have prepared me for that moment. Even today, I have a hard time describing what I felt when I saw her. At the time I wrote this book, my daughter was the same age I was then, and the thought of her feeling what I felt makes me grieve. I was traumatized. I had never seen Mommy like this. So frail. So helpless. I couldn't believe this was my mommy.

One of my family members held me and tried to calm me, but I got worked up every time I looked over at her. Her eyes were half open, and she was hooked up to all kinds of machines. There was a tube down her throat, but her mouth was moving as if she was trying to speak. My sister, who was standing beside the bed holding my mother's hand, kept trying to get me to come closer.

"No!" I protested; I was too frightened to move.

"Mommy wants you to come over here!" my sister snapped at me.

I couldn't do it, but my family members all started pulling me, trying to get me to go closer to her. "Please…please, don't make me go," I pleaded, pulling away.

As I was pulling away from them, I saw Mommy hold out her hand to me.

I could see her mouthing, "Peaches."

She motioned with her hands for me to come to her, but I couldn't. My family must've realized it was too much for me, so they took me out of the room. That was the last time I saw Mommy alive.

Before we left the hospital that day, the doctors took us into a conference room.

"Her brain is no longer functioning properly," they told us. "If she lives, she won't be able to do anything on her own. She will not be able to do simple things like feed and bathe herself. She would be what we call a vegetable."

My sister and Aunt Tricia talked privately. I heard them mention my mother's wishes when it came to life-support. She did not want to be kept on any life-sustaining equipment.

I noticed Aunt Tricia looking over at me while they were talking. Suddenly, I remembered the conversation Mommy and I had when I was about eight or nine years old. She had asked me who I would want to live with if something ever happened to her.

Without thinking, I had said, "Probably Aunt Tricia, but she doesn't like kids."

I didn't really want to live with Aunt Tricia though; she was mean! She didn't have any children, and she always yelled at my cousins and me. I have no idea why I said I would live with her. It just sort of slipped out. I had never even thought about it again.

Meanwhile, I didn't know that Mommy and Aunt Tricia had started making arrangements because they knew she was dying. If I had known why she'd asked, I probably would have said I wanted to live with my sister. Her house was where all the fun was. She had seven children, so I had a bunch of nieces and nephews to play with.

I remember realizing right at that moment that I was about to go live with Aunt Tricia. Everything was happening too fast. *How is Mommy sick all of a sudden? And dying? She was just fine.* Or was she?

I started thinking back over the past couple of months. It made sense now why everyone else was so calm. They all knew she was dying, so they had time to prepare themselves. I was the only person who was caught off guard.

Her health had been rapidly declining over the course of a couple of months. I suppose I was too young to realize she hadn't been herself for quite some time . Although, her never moving from the couch should have been an indication to me that something was wrong.

It had all started a couple of months prior. My stepdad's elderly mom, Grandma Mary, had come to live with us after her caretaker had suddenly died. My stepdad, Mike, was in prison serving time for robbing a bank. When Grandma Mary moved in with us, I had to give her my room and sleep in the living room with my mother. I slept on top of Mommy most nights anyway, so giving up my room was not a problem.

I was excited Grandma Mary was living with us. Both of my biological grandmothers were dead, and I had always wondered what it would be like to actually have a grandma. But, having her with us wasn't as exciting as I thought it would be. All she did was sing ancient hymns, talk to herself, and dip snuff. Snuff was a smokeless tobacco she would swish around her cheeks and spit into a can. It looked and smelled disgusting.

Sometimes, I would sit and try to talk with Grandma Mary, but her Alzheimer's prevented us from having any meaningful conversations. One day, she fell while trying to use the bathroom on her own. When I ran to tell Mommy what happened, she said she would get up in a moment, but she never moved. When a few minutes passed, and Mommy still hadn't moved, I reminded her that Grandma Mary was still on the floor. She kept saying she was coming but never got up. I could hear Grandma Mary calling for help. I went back to the room and tried to help her up myself, but she was too heavy.

I still wonder why it never crossed my mind to call someone for help. I knew how to call 911 in the case of emergency, but for some reason, I didn't. Grandma Mary was never able to get up from the floor, and Mommy never moved from the couch. Ever. I don't even remember Mommy ever going to the bathroom or bathing. No wonder our house smelled so bad.

In the mornings, I was careful not to step on Grandma Mary while getting ready for school. Every day, when I got home from school, both Mommy and Grandma Mary were in the same spot they were in when I left in the morning.

After a few days, Grandma Mary was no longer talking. She lay on the floor, mouth wide open. *She's asleep*, I thought. *She sure is sleeping for a long time.* As days went on, I found myself more and more afraid to step over her, but I had to step over her to get to my dresser where all my clothes were.

Every morning I got up for school, took a bath and got dressed. At school, I was able to eat breakfast and lunch, so I never missed a day of school. At home, the refrigerator and cabinets were all empty except for a few cans of sardines, a jar of coffee, and some teabags, and that was what I had in the evenings. I don't remember what I used to eat on the weekends. I usually spent the night at my friend's house across the street anyway. I always ate well over there.

I'm not sure how many, but days went by before Damion finally came home. Damion wasn't my biological brother; he was actually my cousin. His mother was Aunt Brenda, my mother's younger sister. She died when he was twelve years old, so Mommy took him in as her own. I was just two years old, so I had always known him as my brother. He would disappear for days sometimes weeks. I was so relieved he was there.

"Damion, something is wrong with Grandma Mary," I told him. He went into my room to check on her.

"How long has she been like this?" he asked me. "She's dead!"

"I don't know," I responded. I knew it had been about over a week but I was afraid to tell him.

He called an ambulance, and when they arrived, the first responders confirmed she was dead. They asked Mommy if she knew Grandma Mary had died and she shook her head no. When the coroners did their report they said she had been dead for days. A police detective arrived, and he started looking around our house. I followed him as he looked around. When he got to our freezer, he twisted his face in disgust.

"Oh my God, what have you been eating?" he asked me.

I just hunched my shoulders. *Nothing*, I thought.

The house was filthy and smelly. There was no food, and Grandma Mary's body had been lying on my bedroom floor for days. You can probably guess what happened next.

Police officers put me in the back of their car. I thought they were arresting me until they explained they were taking me because I could no longer live in that house. I cried and begged them to let me stay. Mommy also begged the officers not to take me. And for the very first time, I saw my brother cry as he tried to fight the police officers.

"Get off my little sister! You can't take my little sister!"

He took off his shirt and threw it to the ground. No matter how much he tried, he could not keep the officers from taking me. As we drove off, I looked back and could see him in the street still yelling and screaming. I knew he loved me, but, wow, I didn't know he loved me that much.

When we arrived at the police station, they gave me some

snacks and sat me in an office. I was sitting there eating my snacks when my sister and Aunt Tricia arrived. The officers told them the house needed to be cleaned, and they needed to put food in the house or they would take me away from my mother permanently. They allowed them to take me, so we went back to the house, cleaned up from top to bottom, and went to buy food.

My sister and Aunt Tricia yelled at me, asking why I hadn't called either of them. I couldn't answer because I didn't know. I knew both of their phone numbers, so I don't know why I didn't call them when I was hungry. I don't know why I didn't call them when Grandma Mary fell. I don't know why I didn't call them and tell them Mommy wasn't moving from the couch. I told them I was sorry for not calling and assured them that next time I would.

We spent the next couple of days cleaning the apartment. When the police detective came back out to inspect the apartment, they said I could stay if someone else moved in and helped Mommy. So my Aunt Mae, my mother's aunt, moved in with us. She was the kind of woman that nobody messed with because she didn't play. I used to think she was a gangster. She could be very sweet but would cuss you out in a minute. My mother, Aunt Mae, Damion, and I all stayed in that one-bedroom apartment.

After Aunt Mae moved in, I never suspected that anything was wrong and that my life was about to change forever. It would be a few weeks later that Mommy would be taken to the hospital, never to come back home.

My sister snapped me out of my daydream and asked if I understood everything the doctors said, and I nodded yes.

"We don't want to see Mommy like this, Peaches," my sister said. "We have to let her go."

But, I didn't care about my mother's inability to feed or wash herself; I didn't want her to die! And, I didn't want to live with Aunt Tricia. As we were leaving the hospital, I asked my sister if I could live with her. She said I could come to her house for a few days, but after that I had to go with Aunt Tricia.

I stayed at my sister's house that week and was having so much fun with my nieces and nephews, I almost forgot Mommy was in the hospital dying. My sister and aunts went to the hospital all week, but I never went back. I loved being at my sister's house. I was playing all day and watching cable TV. Life was good...until we got the call.

On a Thursday night, March 28, 1996, my nieces and nephews and I sat watching music videos on a show called "The Box," something we did every night. I remember R Kelly's "Down Low" video was on the screen. It's a video I'll never forget because the machines his girlfriend, Lola, was hooked up to reminded me of the machines Mommy was hooked up to in the hospital. It was a sad video that made me cry every time I saw it. The phone rang and my oldest nephew, James, who was three years older than me, answered the phone. He listened for a minute and then hung up.

As he picked the phone back up and started calling my sister who was down the street at her friend's house, he said, "Sorry, Peaches. The hospital just called. They said Grandma just died."

After he hung up with his mom, he came back to the bed and held me as I cried, telling me it was going to be okay.

~~~

My mother's funeral took place two weeks later on her birthday, April 13. On the morning of the funeral, I had butterflies in my stomach. I had been to a few funerals, but this one was different. I felt sick.

When we pulled up to the funeral home, there were already

a lot of people there. When we lined up to walk in, my niece, Patrice, came beside me and grabbed my arm. We held each other as we walked down the aisle toward the casket. As we got closer, the butterflies in my stomach felt like they multiplied.

When I got to the casket and saw my mother, I collapsed. My uncle, Wayne, picked me up and carried me outside. Every time he took me inside, he had to bring me back out, so he decided it was best to keep me outside. We went to the store, got some chips, and stayed outside until it was time to close the casket.

I decided I would be strong enough to look at her one last time. I stood in front of the casket, looking at her without crying. She did not look like Mommy at all. I hoped it wasn't her, and it was all a big mistake, but when I saw the mark on her ear and looked at her fingers, I knew it was her. I reached over and touched her hand. I couldn't bring myself to kiss her like a couple of other people had. When they closed the casket, I sat down with everyone else.

I couldn't believe how many people were there. I knew Mommy had a lot of friends, but I was surprised when I saw people standing all over the place. People had come in from out of town; some, I hadn't seen in a very long time. Some of the staff from my school had even shown up, including my principal and counselor.

I had been meeting with my school counselor since Mommy died, and she had given me a poem to read at the funeral. Seeing her made me feel so much better. It gave me the strength I needed when it was time for me to read the poem.

"Mothers don't die. They just move in with the Lord and keep house in the sky..." I read. I managed to get through it without crying.

After the funeral, everybody went to Aunt Tricia's apartment. Her place was where everybody went for holidays, Super Bowl parties, and after funerals. This time, though, I was going to my new home. All of our family and friends gathered in Aunt Tricia's one-bedroom apartment, the adults inside and all the kids playing outside. It felt good to be surrounded by so many of our family and friends. But, one by one people started going home, the noise began to die down, and the once crowded living room was now quiet. It was just me, Aunt Tricia, and her husband, Uncle Wayne.

Reality hit me. I didn't want to live with them. I didn't have a room or a bed. All I had was the pullout couch in the living room. I asked them if I could sleep with them, and they said no. I pleaded with them, and they still said no. I hated life at that moment. My Mommy was gone, and I felt like my Aunt Tricia didn't love me. *How could she love me and leave me out here by myself?* I wondered. I felt scared and alone. I just wanted my Mommy back. I cried and pleaded every night for Aunt Tricia and Uncle Wayne to let me sleep with them, and they never gave in. Eventually, as time went on, I began to fall asleep without crying myself to sleep.

I hated living with Aunt Tricia. Every day, I called my sister asking her if I could come live with her. She told me I would get used to it, but I couldn't see how.

"Aunt Tricia is the fun aunt," my sister said. "She is the best. You'll see,"

I couldn't believe my sister had just said that. We couldn't be talking about the same Aunt Tricia! We had a lot of aunts. How could she possibly be the best? I couldn't have any fun. I couldn't have company over or go to any of my friends' houses to spend the night. I couldn't even hug her. At least that's what I thought. I never tried because I figured she wouldn't let me.

I was miserable. I missed Mommy so much, but what kept me encouraged was my belief she was coming back for me. I had been going to church on my own since I was nine years old, and I even went to Bible study every week. When I moved in with Aunt Tricia, she allowed me to keep going as long as the church van came to pick me up, even though it was in my old neighborhood.

In Bible Study, I had learned about Jesus' resurrection, and I remembered one woman telling me that one day we would be reunited with our family members who had died. So, I thought Mommy would be raised from the dead, and we would be reunited soon.

Every time I felt lonely and scared, I reminded myself she was coming back one day. I would often sit and daydream about that day. I pictured it to be like the scene in the movie "Home Alone 2" when MaCaulay Culkin's character turned around, and his mother was standing behind him. Like him, I would run into my mommy's arms and hug her tightly telling her how much I missed her.

I later learned I had misunderstood what I learned in Bible Study. Mommy was not coming back. One night, I dreamt she came back and promised me this time she would take good care of herself. And then I woke up and realized it was only a dream. That dream was the first of many .

My first Christmas without Mommy was the hardest. Christmas had been our favorite holiday, so it had been a big deal in our house. We had always decorated our apartment windows and door, and we'd blasted Christmas music. Mommy had put out the same tree every year, the day after Thanksgiving. It was an artificial tree that was so small we sat it on the window sill of our living room window. She usually had my gifts under the tree as early as one or two weeks before Christmas. I'd walk past my gifts every day wondering what was under that wrapping, the suspense killing me. She had always let me open one gift on Christmas Eve, but I had to wait until Christmas morning to open the rest.

"Please, can I just open **one** more?" I would ask, already knowing her answer.

Our last Christmas together was much different. It was bare under the tree. She told me I wouldn't be getting anything because she didn't have any money. *She's playing*, I thought. I just knew at any moment she would put my gifts under the tree. When Christmas Eve came, I was super excited. I would be able to open one of my gifts! Still, there were no gifts. *Maybe she's just doing things differently,* I thought. I remained hopeful.

I woke up on Christmas morning and ran into the living room. My smile faded when I looked at the tree—still nothing.

"I really didn't get anything?"

"I'm sorry, baby," she said.

I wanted to cry, but I nodded my head and went to the bathroom to brush my teeth.

"Close the door," Mommy told me.

As I was closing the door, I could see her reaching into the closet but I didn't think anything of it. When I came out, she handed me a brand new Barbie doll. My face lit up.

"Thank you, Mommy!" I exclaimed, hugging her tightly. I don't remember which Barbie doll it was or if I'd even asked for one that year, but I was beyond grateful. Just when I'd thought I wasn't getting anything, she surprised me. This would become one of the sweetest memories I have of my mother.

Getting Adjusted

As time went on, I began to adapt to living with Aunt Tricia, even though it was very different than what I was used to. The one thing I liked about living with her was that I ate well every day. She cooked just about every night. When I first moved in, I found myself not wanting to eat too much because I didn't want her to think I was trying to eat all of her food.

"Go ahead and get some more if you want," she said.

Up until I started living with her, I was only eating a little, if anything at all, so it took me awhile to get used to going back for seconds.

Another thing I had to get used to was boundaries. She was a lot stricter than Mommy had been. Mommy had allowed me to have company over and spend the night out whenever I wanted. Aunt Tricia wouldn't allow either.

Mommy had allowed me to play outside all day as long as I didn't go far. Aunt Tricia didn't let me go outside every day, and when she did let me out, I had to stay on the porch. She said no to things Mommy never would've said no to.

By the time I was in middle school, my friends were allowed to go to the movies by themselves, and I was still trying to convince Aunt Tricia to let me ride my bike outside of our neighborhood. I got limited time to talk on the phone, and I would often catch her listening to my conversations. And what was worse, she didn't believe in spending more than twenty dollars on a pair of shoes, nor did she think I needed more than a few outfits. So, I was teased at school about my clothes and also teased because I could never do anything or go anywhere. I couldn't understand why she had such a tight grip on me. It seemed as if all of my friends could do whatever they wanted. Meanwhile, I was confined to our apartment complex.

By the end of middle school and the beginning of my freshman year in high school, I had begun skipping school. It started with skipping classes and leaving early in middle school, and once I got to high school, I was skipping school altogether. I figured since I couldn't go anywhere after school or on the weekends, I might as well have all my fun during school hours. I got caught skipping a couple of times, but it didn't stop me. I would stop for a while, and once my punishment was over, I would skip again.

Aunt Tricia was growing more and more impatient with me. So, one day she popped in at my school to make sure I was there.

On this particular day, I was in school but had decided to skip my last period class and lounge in the school library. They called my name over the intercom, but I never heard it. When I got home that day, she was the angriest I had ever seen. She went on and on about how she was trying to trust me, and how she couldn't believe I had skipped school again. I tried to tell her I was in the school library, but she didn't let me get a word in.

"I'm done. You're going to live with your father!"

I had finally gotten used to living with Aunt Tricia; I didn't want to leave now. We had even moved to a two-bedroom so I now had my own room. I had my own room at my father's house as well but I knew I would be miserable living with him.

I begged for one more chance, but her mind was made up. She had already talked to him, and he was on his way to come pick me up. I pleaded with her, but it did no good. She told me to pack my things, so I did.

When my father got there, he didn't say anything to me. He talked to Aunt Tricia for a few minutes and turned to me and said, "Let's go."

Chapter 2

Hi, Daddy

When my father arrived to pick me up, he was surprisingly calm. I expected him to come through the door and immediately start yelling at me. Instead, he quietly carried my bags. We walked to the station, got on the train, and walked to his house from the station in silence.

I was used to him yelling when he had to come pick me up, so his calmness made me nervous. I had no idea what he was going to do or say when we got to his house. Surprisingly, he didn't say much to me the entire night.

We had done this many times before. Every time I acted up at school, Aunt Tricia sent me to his house. Sometimes, I only went for the weekend; other times, I had to stay for a week or two.

I cried as I unpacked my things. I couldn't believe Aunt Tricia had actually kept her word. She had threatened to send me to my father many times before, but I never thought she would. It crushed me to have to leave my neighborhood and friends behind.

For the first couple of weeks, I called Aunt Tricia every day trying to convince her to let me come back home, but she wasn't trying to hear it. She said I was causing her stress and raising her blood pressure, and with her other health problems, worrying about me was too much for her.

Going to my father's house had not always been an event I dreaded. It used to be exciting. After Mommy died, he started picking me up every other weekend, and we always did something fun, whether it was going to the movies, the zoo, the aquarium, or going out to eat. I loved our weekends. It didn't matter to me that I'd rarely seen him before my mother's death. I was just happy to see him.

It was very awkward at first calling him "Daddy" because I wasn't used to saying it. It took me a long time to be comfortable enough that I didn't have to think about it before I said it. I don't remember what I used to call him when he came to see me as a little girl, or if I ever addressed him at all. I just remember being excited in school all day when I knew he was coming over.

"Your father's coming over after school today," Mommy would say.

All day long, I was filled with excitement, telling all my friends, "My father is coming to see me!" Butterflies in my tummy, I'd practically run home from school.

I'd walk into the apartment and find him standing in my living room.

"Hey, Pumpkin," he'd say.

That was his nickname for me even though everyone else called me Peaches. I'd run to him holding out my arms for him to pick me up. I felt like I was on top of the world when he put me up on his shoulders. It could be months before I saw him again, so every time he visited, I was all over him.

After my tenth birthday party, I didn't see him again until my mother's funeral.

A few days after my mother's funeral, he called me and told me he had a surprise for me.

"Hello," an unfamiliar voice said.

"Hello?" I said. "Who is this?"

"Terry."

I couldn't believe it! I was hearing my brother's voice for the very first time.

I had known about Terry my entire life but had never met or talked to him. He was ten years older than I was and lived out of state.

From the time my father told me I had a brother on his side, I had always asked, "When am I going to meet him?" And now here he was on the telephone! I was so nervous; I didn't know what to say. He asked me how old I was and how I was doing in school.

"Ten," I told him. "I'm doing good," I said nervously, my smile so wide I'm sure it touched my ears.

"I can't wait to meet you," he said.

And I couldn't wait to meet him. I used to daydream about meeting him and imagine us playing, him carrying me around on his back. For a long time, I imagined what he was like. I no longer had to imagine when the day came that I finally met him. He had recently moved back to D.C. and was living with my father. When I went to visit him, it was also the first time I'd ever been to my father's house.

"Go ahead and look around," my father said. "Terry's upstairs."

I walked upstairs, and there he was. I ran to him and hugged him tightly. My dream had come true. I was finally meeting my big brother. He looked nothing like the picture I had in my mind. He looked a lot like my father, just a younger, more handsome version.

I remember thinking, *my brother is cute! All my friends are going to have a crush on him!*

We sat for a while and talked, getting to know each other. After that, I called Terry just about every day. I was no longer nervous; I felt like I'd known him my whole life.

I learned he was a writer and a poet. I shared with him my own love for writing short stories and poetry.. He was so different from my brothers on my mother's side, who were always in and out of prison. I don't know why, but I had imagined him to be the same. But, he wasn't. He was educated, kind, and soft-spoken.

He surprised me one day as we were getting off the phone.

"I'll talk to you later. I love you," he said.

"I love you too!" I was so happy to hear my brother loved me.

I was still learning to cope with the loss of my mother, but this new relationship with my brother gave me something to look forward to. His fiancée was pregnant with a baby boy, so I would soon have a brand new nephew and I couldn't wait.

Sometime after, Aunt Tricia told me she had received a call from my father saying he wanted to see me. On the drive over, she was quiet, but I didn't think anything of it. When we got to my father's house, he motioned for me to sit with him on the couch.

"Pumpkin," he started, "Terry got robbed a few nights ago and was stabbed."

"Okay..." I nodded, waiting for him to finish.

"Terry is dead."

Dead? How could my brother be dead? I'd just talked to him a few days ago.

My father told me Terry was the victim of a random attack. He just happened to be at the wrong place at the wrong time, stabbed by some gang members who had vowed to kill the very next person they saw. That person happened to be my brother. For a moment, I sat and listened silently to my father. Suddenly, I burst into tears. I'd waited so long to meet my brother, and we had only been able to see each other once.

I kept thinking about the last time we'd talked when he'd told me he loved me. Now, he was gone. *Why did this have to happen?* I just didn't get it. He was such a good person and never did anything to hurt anyone. He was about to get married and become a father. It had only been five months since Mommy had died and now my brother was dead too. *Why me?*

~~~

Things began changing after a few years. My father stopped calling me Pumpkin and started calling me terrible names. We were no longer doing fun things when I came over on the weekends. Most of the time, I was only at his house because I had done something wrong. His house was my punishment, which was what hurt so much when I had to live with him permanently. Aunt Tricia knew of some of the mean things he had said to me, so I didn't understand why she would make me live with him.

Things got worse when I moved in, and I could no longer go "home" to get away from him. He started making little comments about my mother. The first time I heard him say something bad about her, it caught me off guard. I couldn't believe he would talk negatively about Mommy right in front of me. But as time went on, the comments only got worse and became more frequent. He often told me I would turn out just like she had.   I always wondered if he meant I would be a drug addict and alcoholic like my mother had been. Or did he mean I would get AIDS and die? Whatever he meant, I didn't like it.

He told me he was drunk when I was conceived. He said Mommy tricked him into getting pregnant, and it never would've happened if he was sober.

Hearing those words made me feel like he didn't want me and like I was a burden on him.

It wasn't enough to insult my mother; he began insulting me. He often called me ugly, always pointing out how big my forehead was. He called me "Bitch" as if it was my first name. "Big forehead monkey-looking fucker" was his favorite name for me.

He would say all of these hurtful things and, in the next breath, tell me he loved me and would die for me. I had a hard time believing him; sometimes, he seemed to hate me. He drank just about every night, and when he was drunk, he transformed into an angry man. He would sit up all night drinking, listening to music, and ranting.

Some nights, he called me downstairs just to yell at me. I'd stand there while he went on and on, his breath reeking of alcohol and his spit striking my face as he spoke. I learned to pretend I was asleep as soon he began drinking. I'd lie there praying he wouldn't call me downstairs. Many nights I cried myself to sleep.

Some mornings I woke up to find him sitting in the same spot, still talking and cursing. There were countless mornings I woke up to find our front door open, with my father passed out on the couch. I thank God for His protection because anyone could have come in, robbed us, and done whatever they wanted to us both.

When he was sober, he wasn't as mean; he was actually kind at times. He talked and laughed with me like we were friends. One time he joked about how his friends referred to him as "warden," because he was so strict; but there was nothing funny about it to me. I felt like I was in jail every day, and it was no laughing matter. I wanted to run away, but I was too afraid of what might happen if I got caught and had to come back.

My sister, Kelly, now living in Richmond, Virginia was waiting for "the call" so she could buy my bus ticket. After years of telling me I couldn't live with her, she finally said yes when I told her how my father was treating me. All I needed to do was let her know when I was ready, but fear kept me from leaving. I'd pack and then unpack. Pack. Unpack. I believed my father when he said he would hurt me, so I stayed put...until the end of my senior year of high school, right before I graduated. My "breath of fresh air" got me out of there.

My Breath of Fresh Air

I refer to my "breath of fresh air" as the woman who came into my life when I was eleven years old. I was at my father's house one weekend, sitting on the couch watching TV, when I heard a knock at the front door. My father had already told me he was expecting company, so I opened the door and let her in.

"Hi, come on in," I said waving.

"Hi, I'm Paula," she said, smiling as she walked inside.

She is so pretty, I thought. It was hard to believe she and my father were the same age because she looked so young. Before she'd arrived, my father had already told me their story. They had been friends since they were six years old. Their mothers lived next door to each other for years. She and my father had grown up together, dated off and on, and remained good friends. They had lost contact over the years, so this would be their first time seeing one another in a very long time. I liked Paula right away because she was so warm and inviting. She hugged me and talked to me while my father was upstairs getting ready. He was taking his time, making sure he looked and smelled nice.

When he finally came down, I watched them hug tightly, and then they sat on the couch. They must've talked for hours. I was sad when it was time for her to leave, asking her to stay a little while longer. She assured me she'd be back soon. I don't remember how my hair was at the time, but I'm sure it was probably a mess, because she promised me she would come back in a few days to braid it for me.

"Okay," I said, only half believing her. People were always telling me they were going to do something and never did it, so I expected the same from her.

My face lit up when she arrived a few days later, just as she'd said she would, with all the supplies to braid my hair. She sat on the couch; I sat on the floor between her legs, and for the next few hours, she braided my hair. Even at eleven years old, I knew how to be thankful when someone did something for me that they didn't have to do.

From that moment on, I felt like I got a breath of fresh air every time she came over. It was always just my father and me, so it was always nice when someone else was there with us, particularly Paula. I liked the feeling of having her there.

She instantly took me in like I was one of her own, teaching me how to be a young lady from personal hygiene to making sure I made my bed every morning. When I got my monthly cycle for the first time, she bought me a vanity bag packed with pads, deodorant, a bar of soap, Ibuprofen, and an extra pair of panties. She told those were the necessities every lady should carry.

She had had four daughters of her own, and five grandchildren. When she introduced me to them she said, "These are your sisters, and those are your nieces and nephews."

I never really knew what to call her. When talking about her to people, I referred to her as my stepmother, but she and my dad weren't married. Referring to her as my father's friend was a major understatement as she was much more to me than that. Godmother sounded like an understatement as well, as the term is overused. I could never bring myself to call her, or anyone else, "Mommy," because it felt like I was betraying my mother. So, I stuck with calling her by her first name.

Paula would come get me on weekends and take me to one of her daughter's houses to get a break from my father. She tried to get me away from him as much as possible, especially after I moved in with him permanently. Paula and my father often argued because of his drinking and rage. He had become verbally abusive toward her as well, and she finally decided she couldn't take it anymore.

Paula sat me down in my room one night and told me she could no longer deal with my father, but she assured me she would always be there for me, and she was. Every graduation—elementary, middle, and high school—she made sure my hair and attire were on point. For my middle and high school proms, she got my hair done, bought my dresses, and drove my friends and me to both.

When I was crowned Miss Rambler, one of my high school's homecoming queens, she showed up just as I thought I wouldn't have a car to ride in for the homecoming parade. Parade goers were oohing and aahing as we rode by; not at me, but at her shiny black Mercedes Benz with its twenty-inch rims. I stood out of the sunroof, smiling and waving proudly.

Half-way through my senior year of high school, Paula moved me out of my father's house. I had been going with her most weekends and returning back home on Sundays. But one Sunday, she decided I wasn't going back. She could see the damage he was doing to my mind, my emotions, and even my body.

I had gained a significant amount of weight in my junior and senior years of high school, because eating was one of the ways I dealt with depression. I didn't know I was depressed; I just knew I was sad every day and eating made me feel better. Apparently, Paula noticed. She could see I was on a downward spiral. I hadn't realized those "weekend getaways" were her way of gradually moving me out.

My father never asked me when I was coming back, and I never wanted to go back. Shortly after I left, the house went into foreclosure, and he had to move in with a friend. I was sad about losing our home but happy I was finally *free*. At least, I thought I was. I would never have to live with my father again, but I was not free from him at all.

Although I was now physically free, I was still emotionally and mentally bound by his words, the lies he'd engrained into me that I believed to be my truth. *I'm ugly. I'm dumb. An accident. I'm going to end up just like my mother.*

My father's thoughts about me became my own. I dealt with my issues the best way I knew how—with sex and marijuana. The combination of the two created an imitation of love that I knew, deep down, wasn't the real thing, but it was enough. It only lasted a moment, and I was often worse off after than I was before, but it didn't matter.

By the time I graduated from high school, I was addicted to that moment, and a childhood addiction I'd grown out of resurfaced.

Bound

I knew as early as three years old how to bring myself sexual pleasure. I didn't know what I was doing, except giving myself that "feeling," which I achieved by rubbing something against me or rubbing my private parts against another person's private parts. I would rub up against almost every boy or girl I played with, whether it was a family member or one of my friends. Sometimes, the other child had already been exposed to this form of playing, but most of the time I was introducing it to them for the very first time.

I was four years old the first time I got caught. I had taken off my pants and was rubbing against a little boy Mommy was babysitting. She walked in on me and demanded I tell her what I was doing. I sat there crying, not knowing what to say. She grabbed her belt and gave me a spanking I'll never forget. It was, however, the first of many spankings, as I got caught often, but the spankings didn't stop me from pleasuring myself. If I wasn't doing it every day, it was every other day, sometimes, a few days in between. For years, it was as ordinary as playing with my dolls. It was something I just *did*.

After Mommy died, I stopped. I'm not sure how I was able to stop so abruptly. Perhaps the trauma I experienced from losing her made me forget all about it. I didn't even think about it again until I was fifteen years old when I spent the night at a family member's house. There were many kids there, family and some of our friends. We older kids were responsible for watching the smaller children, since the adults had gone out. We were spread out between two bedrooms, some sleeping on the bed and some of us on the floor.

In the middle of the night, I woke up to someone touching me. I had been sleeping in a small corner by myself and had never even felt him lie beside me.

He was a friend of the family who came over often. When I realized what was happening, I didn't stop him as I liked what he was doing. He touched me and did things to me until I experienced that familiar feeling. What had been lying dormant for five years reawakened, and now it was stronger than ever.

Once again, I was addicted to bringing myself sexual pleasure. It wasn't until I was in a sex education class in school when I learned what that feeling actually was. I had heard the term orgasm many times before but never knew it was what I was experiencing.

My mind had become consumed with sex, from watching pornography, reading erotic books, to even writing some of my own. It wasn't long before I wanted to do some of those things I watched, read about, and wrote about, but even more than that, I yearned to experience the love I read about in fairy tales.

There was nothing special about my first time having sex, nor was there anything special about the boy I experienced it with. He didn't know it, but he was just helping me cover up a lie. The boy

I actually liked, an older boy named Phil, believed I was already experienced. Trying to impress him, I had told him I wasn't a virgin. Phil often pressured me, telling me that if I loved him, I would have sex with him. Wanting to prove my love, I decided I was going to have sex with him. I knew he'd realize I had been lying, so I decided I needed to lose my virginity and gain some experience before we slept together for the first time.

You may be reading this and wondering, *what were you thinking?* Believe me, I realize now how foolish my thinking was. But I would have done just about anything in the name of "love." I wanted to show Phil I loved him, and, more than anything, I wanted him to love me back. I believed having sex with him was the only way. One evening, I told my father I would be staying at school for an after school program. Instead, I was at a boy's house, a boy I barely knew, giving away my virginity.

~~~

If only someone had told me how precious my purity,
And warned me of the consequences of going down this road
prematurely.
If only someone had told me how I would later cringe at
the thought of losing my virginity to a boy I never really knew;
If only someone had told me sex does not equal love,
and just because a boy has sex with you doesn't mean he loves you.

~~~

The boy I lost my virginity to was the first of many undeserving boys to whom I gave my body while I was in high school. I eventually got with Phil, but that relationship didn't last long. Apparently, I wasn't the only girl he "loved." So, I was on to the next, and then the next.

The majority of the time, the sex wasn't even enjoyable, but I felt compelled to do it. A part of me felt like I was getting back at my father whenever I had sex. He hadn't the slightest idea I had boys in the house all the time. I experienced a false sense of empowerment, because even though my father controlled every aspect of my life, he couldn't control what I did with my body. There were many times I thought to myself, *I'm gonna show him.* What I didn't realize was that it wasn't my father I was hurting. I was hurting myself.

Chapter 3

Pregnant and Homeless

After graduating from high school, I lived with Paula for awhile. I ended up getting into some trouble so she thought it was best that I go back to live with Aunt Tricia. When I first asked Aunt Tricia if I could come back, I thought I would have to beg, but I was surprised when she quickly said yes. It felt so good to be back home. It had been four years since she had sent me to live with my father, although I had visited and stayed over many times.

The first thing Aunt Tricia told me was that I needed to find a job. I didn't know if going to college was going to be an option for me at that point, as I had barely made it out of high school. It wasn't until the last month of school that I got myself together and made up all the work I had missed.

The night before graduation, I wrote an essay for my English teacher so I could bring my F up to a D-. I turned it in the next morning and walked across the stage a couple hours later.

I was so over school but had always dreamed of becoming a doctor. I had known since I was a little girl I wanted to take care of people who were sick, so I thought about going to community college and transferring to a university later.

When I took the placement test, I scored very low in math and discovered I would need to take two developmental math classes before I could take a math class that would count toward my credits. Math had always been my weakest subject, and the thought of taking those two classes and knowing there was more to come, intimidated me.

So, I began searching for careers that would allow me to work in the medical field without all the math. I found a course for medical assisting that was a little less than a year, with very little math, and it was all hands-on training. I was learning how to do everything I always dreamed of doing—checking vital signs, drawing blood, giving shots, doing EKGs, and learning how to give CPR. I had the best grades in my class, all A's, and I never missed one day. I had never loved school so much. I went to class in the mornings and worked in a clothing store in the evenings and on the weekends.

My boyfriend at the time, Sean, picked me up from work most nights. I dated Sean for a few months and thought I was in love. I wasn't the only one "in love" with him, though. His child's mother constantly called him, trying to get him back. I wanted to believe him when he said she was crazy, and he hadn't slept with her as she claimed. But, deep down, I knew she wasn't as crazy as he made her out to be.

He had given her the same hope he had given me. Tired of all the drama, I left him. Shortly after our breakup, I ran into his best friend and learned he had been shot and killed.

That night, I put "Diary" by Alicia Keys on repeat and cried myself to sleep. Although we had parted on bad terms, that song reminded me of our good times.

Once I completed my classes, I was hired in the gynecology office where I had completed my externship. I was one of the few people who got hired from an externship while others were left to find employment on their own. The office was near the store, so I worked both jobs. At nineteen, it was pretty easy for me to juggle two jobs while still hanging out all night with my friends.

Aunt Tricia didn't care what I did as long as I paid my portion of the rent on time. She didn't even care when I came in the house smelling like marijuana. She actually got a kick out of teasing me when I came home high. Because she had been so strict when I was a child, it surprised me she was okay with everything I was doing then.

"You're grown," she often told me, "Just don't wake me up when you come in late, and don't bring no babies in here." I soon found out she was serious when she said that.

One evening when I was working the cash register at my store, a guy walked in who caught my interest. There were two other people with him, another guy and a lady. He wasn't really my type physically, but there was something about him I liked. When he got up to the register to pay for his items, I asked him if the woman with him was his girlfriend.

"No, that's my little sister," he said smiling.

So, I wrote down my number and gave it to him. His name was Cal, and he called me the next day. While talking to him, I realized he was the complete opposite of what I usually liked. Aside from the fact Cal wasn't my type physically, he was very quiet. I had always liked outgoing guys who were loud and funny, but there was still something about him that drew me to him. He was older than me by nine years and had his own place so I was impressed. And I figured since he was older and he stayed to himself, he would treat me right. We got close very fast. After our first date, I saw him just about every day.

Sometimes, I stayed at his house for days at a time. I had always been conscious about the possibility of pregnancy and sexually transmitted diseases, but, for some reason, neither ever crossed my mind when I was with Cal. While I was adamant about using protection with previous partners, I never thought about it with him. The majority of our time was spent in his bedroom, and when we weren't in the bedroom, I was wondering when we were going back.

I'm not sure why I was surprised when I found out I was pregnant in March, and I had just met him in January. At the rate we were going, it was bound to happen. I used to daydream about having a baby, but I never thought it would happen so soon.

I was happy but terrified at the same time. I worried about what Aunt Tricia would say. I managed to hide my pregnancy from her for the first few weeks, but it got harder to keep it a secret as my morning sickness got worse. I couldn't keep leaving the house every time I had to throw up. I couldn't find the right way to tell her, so I handed her the note from my doctor with my pregnancy test result and my estimated due date.

I stood in silence as she read the note. She stared at me for a moment in disbelief before she started yelling at me. It had been a long time since I had seen her so angry. She picked up the phone and started dialing. I figured she was calling one of my aunts.

"You won't believe this!" she screamed into the phone. She went on to tell her the news.

A few minutes later, she handed me the phone. It was my Aunt Kema. She tried to talk me into getting rid of the baby, but there was no way I was having an abortion.

"Did you get rid of your baby?" I asked her, referring to my cousin.

"No."

"Well don't tell me to get rid of mine," I told her before handing the phone back to Aunt Tricia.

After Aunt Tricia got off the phone with Aunt Kema, she told me how disappointed she was. She told me if I didn't have an abortion, I had to find a new place to stay. Assuming she just needed time to cool off, I decided to go back to Cal's house for a few days. This time, however, when we talked about my pregnancy, he no longer seemed happy. He went on about how he wasn't ready for another child.

His attitude had changed, and I noticed his tone was now different when he talked to me. Instead of being the sweet, soft-spoken man I knew him to be, he was very short with me and cold. After a few days, I'd had enough. I was very sick, and the constant arguing made me feel worse.

I packed all the stuff I had at his house and asked him to take me home. He dropped me off, but when I got to the door and inserted my key, it didn't work. I tried again, and still, the lock wouldn't budge. It then dawned on me that Aunt Tricia had changed the locks. I knocked on the door, asking if she could let me in.

"No," she said through the door. "I told you, you are not bringing any babies in my house."

My heart sank. She was serious about wanting me to leave. Cal had already pulled off. I tried calling his phone to come back and get me, but he didn't pick up. With my bags in hand, I walked down the street to my friend Kenyatta's house. We had been friends since we were four years old, so her mother welcomed me with open arms. She said I could stay there until I found a permanent place to live. I was very grateful to her for opening up her home to me. She gave me some blankets and sat a bucket beside the couch where I slept.

Days went by, and I was losing weight rapidly as I couldn't keep anything down, not even water. I had already been in the hospital twice, diagnosed with hyperemesis. I had to receive fluids through an IV because I was severely dehydrated. I had quit my job at the store as soon as my morning sickness had started but kept my day job at the doctor's office. I had a great office manager who allowed me to take off as much as I needed.

I was confined to Kenyatta's couch for days before I was able to finally get up and look for a program that could assist me with housing. Every program I contacted was either full or only provided services to mothers who had already had their babies. The very last place I visited suggested I call Covenant House of Washington, a nonprofit organization for teens and young adults.

"Here," the front desk receptionist said as she handed me a

piece of paper with a phone number. "Covenant House has a shelter and an independent living program. They should be able to help you."

I said a quick prayer before I called and sure enough, they had a bed for me at their youth shelter. At 5:00 that evening, a van came to pick me up.

Two men got out and helped me with my bags.

For a second, I almost changed my mind. I wondered what I was getting myself into, but then I figured I should at least give it a try. I thought it couldn't be any worse than my current situation. After riding for what seemed like forever, we pulled up to the building that would become my home for the next three months.

The youth shelter at Covenant House was nothing like I expected. Whenever I thought of a shelter, I imagined a large room with rows of cots. This place was an apartment building with dorm-like rooms. There was also an office for the residential advisors, or RAs, as we called them.

Once I got registered with the office, my RA walked me to my room. There were two twin size beds, two dressers, a closet and a small bathroom. It wasn't like home, but it was pretty decent.

"You're lucky;" my RA said, "you get a room to yourself. But that can change at any moment, so enjoy it while it lasts." She smiled as she closed the door to leave.

I was unpacking my things when someone knocked and told me to come down for dinner. During dinner I got to see how many other people were there. There were a bunch of girls and a few guys, ranging from age seventeen to twenty-one. Most of the girls had babies; a few girls were pregnant.

Being the new girl, I was bombarded with questions:

"Did you get put out?"

"What neighborhood you from?"

"Where's the father?"

I wasn't bothered by all the questions. I just assumed every new person went through it. After dinner, we went into the TV room for a while before going to bed.

The next morning, I woke up to banging on my door. It was the RAs letting me know it was 6:00 a.m. and time to get up. It seemed like I had just fallen asleep. All the residents were required to leave every day at 8:00 a.m., and we could return no earlier than 3:00 p.m. This was how they ensured we were using our time wisely. The goal was for us to get ourselves together while we were there, not sleep all day. Those of us who had jobs were to leave out every day and go to work; those who did not have jobs were expected to leave out every day and look for work.

Every time I went to work, though, I had to run to the bathroom every fifteen minutes to throw up. No matter how well I was doing, I got sick the moment I walked in the door of my job. I would go in, only to be sent home within the first couple of hours. Usually, I would go sleep at one of my friends' houses since I couldn't go back to the shelter too early. After a few more hospital visits, my doctor put me on bedrest and I was able to stay at the shelter during the day.

~~~

Cal completely stopped answering my calls. I had gone to his house a few times, but he would never answer the door. I even called his best friend's phone. He said he hadn't heard from him either. I would have believed him, if they hadn't lived in the same house.

When I told him I knew he was lying, he got mad, and, in the midst of our argument, he told me Cal had other children. I only knew about Cal's three-year-old son, so this was news to me. According to the best friend, he had an older daughter and possibly more. I couldn't believe what I was hearing.

Cal had seemed like such a good guy, but he turned out to be a liar. I felt stupid. I thought I was smart to date an older man, a man who seemed so different from the street boys I usually dated.

After talking to his best friend, my hurt turned to anger. Wanting to confront Cal, I went to his house again. I decided this would be the final time.

When I didn't get an answer, I sat on the porch, waiting. He never showed. I sat crying, wondering if he was inside ignoring me. I was tempted to pick up a rock and throw it through the window but decided against it because I knew the noise would bring attention my way. Instead, I used the end of my umbrella to engrave obscenities into the door. He and everyone else would see it. While I knew I was wrong for what I did, it felt good doing it. I walked away smiling.

~~~

While at Covenant House, I noticed members of the staff often referred to us as "homeless youth." I had a difficult time accepting that word. I didn't feel like a "homeless youth." When I thought of homeless people, I pictured people sleeping outside on park benches, at bus stops, and on sidewalks, and I wasn't sleeping in any of those places.

When I expressed my frustration over the term to my RA she asked me, "Why are you here?"

"My aunt put me out of her house when she found out I was pregnant," I told her.

"If you leave, do you have a place to go?" she asked.

"No," I replied.

"Kendra, that means you are homeless," she said.

That conversation with my RA changed my perspective. I was *homeless*. We all were homeless. Some of us were put out by family members. Some had been homeless their entire lives, and some had left home because they no longer wanted to follow their parents' rules.

As I was approaching my three-month mark, I realized my time at the shelter was winding down. Three months was the maximum time we were allowed to stay in the shelter. By then, we needed to either have a place of our own or apply to one of their extended housing programs. My RA encouraged me to apply to the independent living program. It was an eighteen-month program, but because I was pregnant, I could stay for twenty-four months. I filled out the paperwork, got a background check, obtained my references, and everything else I needed, and moved in within a month of applying.

I was happy to be in an apartment and felt like I was on my own. There were still rules to follow, but we had much more freedom than we had at the crisis center. We were on our own when it came to buying food, toiletries, and anything else we needed. Each month, we sat down with our RA and went over a budget. The amount of rent we paid was based on our income, minus our household expenses. This money was put into a savings account for us to get back after we completed the program.

~~~

At six months pregnant, my belly finally began to show. Even though it was still very small, I was happy to show off my baby bump and put the rumors to rest. People had started questioning whether or not I was really pregnant. Another pregnant girl in the program started a rumor I wasn't really pregnant. I was farther along than she was, but her belly was growing faster than mine.

She insisted I'd made it all up. Somehow, my stomach had remained flat during my first five months. Perhaps, it was because of the weight loss I experienced due to the sickness. By the time I was in my eighth month, my belly seemed to grow overnight.

During my last few months of pregnancy, I was bored out of my mind. Although I was supposed to be on bedrest, I had tried to return to work again later in my pregnancy thinking the sickness had subsided. Again, I got sick the moment I walked into the office.

The doctor I worked for said to me, "Stay home. Your job will still be here after you have the baby."

So, I watched TV all day and slept. In the evenings, I sat in the RAs office watching movies. Their office was in an apartment building next to my building, so sometimes I was there up until 1:00 or 2:00 a.m. This was my routine for the remainder of my pregnancy, and they never complained.

The closer I got to the end of my pregnancy, the more nervous and excited I became. I was excited about meeting my baby but afraid of all the things that could go wrong. I worried about the cord getting wrapped around her little neck. I worried about her coming out with breathing or heart problems, and the possibility of one of us dying during child birth.

I prayed every day I would have a healthy baby. I couldn't wait to love my daughter. Some nights, I sat on my bed cradling a onesie in my arms imagining it was her. I'd rock the onesie and play my song for her, "For You I Will" by Monica. *"I will cross the ocean for you. I will go and bring you the moon. I will be your hero, your strength, anything you need. I will be the sun in your sky. I will light your way for all time. Promise you. For you, I will."*

One night, I got a call I wasn't expecting. It was Aunt Tricia. She called to tell me she was cooking Thanksgiving dinner and wanted me to come.

Hiding my excitement, I told her I'd be there. It had been months since I had talked to her. The only time we talked was when I first moved into the independent living program and picked up the rest of my belongings from her apartment.

Many times during my pregnancy, I had wished I could see her and talk to her. And now she was reaching out to me! I was just happy to be talking to her again. Thanksgiving Day couldn't come quickly enough. I had missed her so much.

We talked, laughed, ate and had a good time. It felt so good to be home, sleeping in my old bed that night. As good as it felt, I knew it was just for the night.

While I missed being home, I never felt an urge to ask if I could come back. I had a great thing going at Covenant House. I was looking forward to saving my money and moving out on my own. I was due to have the baby within a couple of weeks, and she promised she would be the first person to visit when I got home from the hospital.

Thirty-six Hours of Labor!

Saturday, one day after my due date I started feeling pain. The pain was mild and felt like menstrual cramps, so I ignored it and continued watching TV. When the pain came back, I wondered if they could be contractions. I had always heard contractions were excruciating, so I thought these couldn't be contractions. I called my sister, Mari , and told her what I was feeling.

"Girl," she said, "those are contractions. I'm on my way."

She picked me up and took me to the hospital. Because I was full term, I was taken straight to labor and delivery. A nurse hooked me up to a monitor and confirmed I was contracting about every fifteen minutes. I had only dilated two centimeters, so they told me I needed to go back home.

Instead of taking me back to my apartment, Mari took me to Paula's house. It was my first time seeing her since I left her house.

When I had called to tell her I was pregnant, she promised me she would be there when it was time for me to have the baby. And she was.

The contractions continued all through the night and got stronger and more frequent.

"It's gotta be time now. We need to get you to the hospital." Paula rushed me to the hospital.

Again, they hooked me to a monitor and told me I was in labor, but because I hadn't dilated anymore and my water hadn't broken, there was nothing they could do. They said it could be hours since it was my first pregnancy. The contractions were more annoying than they were painful. They were coming every few minutes, and I just wanted them to stop. Every time I got comfortable, another one would hit me.

After leaving the hospital, we went to the mall to do some shopping. Yes, shopping! Paula insisted the walking would be good for me. As we were shopping, the contractions became more and more painful. We went from store and store, and I remember looking at Mari and Paula as they shopped and thought how lucky they were because they weren't experiencing my pain .

They did know my pain, though. Paula had gone through it four times, and Mari had gone through it twice. I was miserable. I wished my water would just break already.

That night was another sleepless night for me. The pain had me tossing and turning until morning. I joked about my contractions feeling like a one-two punch. They were coming strong and fast. The first punch was bearable, sort of like a menstrual cramp. It was the second punch that was excruciating. This pain immediately followed the menstrual cramp-like pain, but it started inside of my lower back and seemed to move throughout my entire body. If it weren't for that second punch, I would say contractions are a piece of cake. When I got up the next morning, I had lost my mucous plug.

"Come on!" Paula said. "We are going back to the hospital, and we are not leaving."

For the third time, we rushed to the hospital. This time, we weren't going anywhere, no matter what they said. I got hooked up to the monitor and was contracting every few minutes. This time, when they checked me, I had dilated four centimeters.

Finally, they admitted me but instructed me to walk around the hospital so my water would break. So we walked, and we walked. And, we walked some more. Every time I felt a contraction, I walked faster instead of doubling over in pain. Speed walking eased the pain. People stopped in the halls and encouraged me as I walked.

Paula told me she had never seen anyone so calm while in labor. I never screamed. I never cried out. I just walked through the contractions. After walking around the hospital for what seemed like forever, my water still hadn't broken.

When I got back to labor and delivery, I had dilated seven centimeters. Walking had helped tremendously. Now, I was ready for some pain medicine. I had been dealing with this pain for almost three days, and I couldn't take it anymore. I got an epidural, which hurt worse than the contractions. When getting the epidural, the doctor instructs you to remain absolutely still, but if you've had a contraction I'm sure you know that it's impossible to be still when you have a sharp pain shooting through your back.

Once the epidural kicked in, I no longer felt any pain. I smiled as I saw the contractions on the screen because I felt nothing. My water never broke on its own, so they had to break it. Once they broke my water, the contractions got stronger, and I could feel them again. Then it was finally time to push. It seemed like I was pushing forever.

Paula and my father were in the room with me coaching me as I pushed. My Kyelia was born at 8:00 p.m. on Monday,

December 12, 2005. She was six pounds, three ounces and nineteen inches long.

When I heard my baby cry, I breathed a sigh of relief. They put Kyelia in my arms for a few moments before taking her to clean her up. They brought her back to me a little while later, and we all took turns holding her and looking at her.

Early the next morning, the nurse brought Kyelia to me so I could begin breastfeeding. After feeding her, I held her and stared down at her. I couldn't

believe my baby was finally here. I looked over her entire little body, examining her. I was happy to see that she had all her fingers and toes. The best moment was when I held her up in the air and kissed her little mouth. She sucked on my lip, and it was the best feeling ever. I was in love.

~~~

After three days of labor, with contractions five minutes apart,
At 8:00 p.m. on a Monday night a little girl stole my heart.
I cried when I saw her; my baby was finally here.
They put her in my arms; I looked down and said, "Hello, Kyelia."
She was so little; I was afraid I would break her.
Nervous about doing something wrong, I asked the nurses to take her.
The next morning they brought her to me so I could nurse her.
Looking in her little face, I no longer feared hurting her.
They said there's a chance she wouldn't immediately latch on,
But that I should be patient and eventually she'll catch on.
Like it was yesterday, I remember our first kiss.
Her little eyes seemed to be scanning the room as she sucked on my lip.
It took us a little while to get used to each other.
She was new to the world, and I was new to being a mother.
We eventually begin to see eye to eye.

Whenever she needed something, all she had to do was cry.
To her, I rushed to make it all better,
Whether it was feeding her, rocking her, or changing her stinky pamper.
All these years later, I'm still in disbelief,
But God I thank You so much for entrusting her to me.

~~~

Caring for my baby came so naturally to me. It was no longer just about me. I now had another life to look after. This tiny person depended on me to keep her fed, clean, and safe.

I admit, it was scary at first, but I never knew I could love so much. The fear I had during my pregnancy didn't compare to the fear I felt once she was out in the world. So many things went through my mind. I was afraid of someone kidnapping her or losing her to sudden infant death syndrome. I woke up many nights, just to put my hand on her back to make sure she was still breathing.

When it came time to put her in daycare, I cried every day for the first couple of weeks. I wondered, *what if they are hurting my baby.* I'd never know. I had to work, so I didn't have a choice. All I could do was pray they were taking good care of her. I left home every morning while it was still dark, and sometimes it would be dark when I got back home in the evenings.

My daughter was one of the first children dropped off at her daycare center in the mornings, and one of the last children picked up in the evenings. I got letters from the center every week notifying me that leaving my baby in childcare for ten hours every day was a form of neglect, but catching three buses and having to start work at 8:00 a.m. left me no choice.

Asking her father for help wasn't an option. After Kyelia was born, I'd had to show up at Cal's job and act a fool just to get him to visit her. I thought once he saw our daughter for the first time he would fall in love and want to be in her life forever. I was wrong.

After cursing him out and getting physical with him on numerous occasions, the owner of the club where Cal worked security told me I couldn't come back. He later got fired, and I had no other way of getting in contact with him. I often cried and beat myself up for being so stupid. *If only I hadn't said anything to him when I first saw him*, I thought. But, then I would look at my daughter's little face and feel guilty for wishing I hadn't met her father. If I hadn't met him, I never would have had her, and the thought of never having her saddened me even more.

When I found out Cal hadn't seen either of his other children in years, I knew my daughter would be no exception. I had to accept he didn't want to be in her life; he only visited her a few times before disappearing completely from her life. I was going to be raising her on my own. I became determined to work hard and give my daughter the life I'd never had.

Giving up wasn't an option. Many days I got caught in the pouring rain, walked home in the cold, and caught the bus with both hands full of grocery bags—all with my daughter strapped to my chest in a harness. I carried her in that harness until she was well past a year old. I often had back pain as a result, but it was much easier than pushing her in the stroller, especially when I had to walk up the hill to the laundromat. There was no way I could push a stroller and a laundry cart full of clothes at the same time.

It was a struggle, but in my mind, I was just doing what I had to do. I had never driven before, so I took lessons, got my driver's license, and bought my first car. Life got so much easier once I had a car.

~~~

I was twenty-one years old when I moved out of Covenant House's transitional living program and into the real world. I had used my time in transitional living wisely, taking advantage of everything they had to offer. I knew once I left, I would never get this kind of opportunity again. The money I had been paying each month had been put into a savings account and had accrued interest.

I had about $4,000 saved, which was more than enough money to pay the security deposit on my new apartment and to buy furniture. I had come such a long way. Just two years prior, I had been pregnant, alone, and had nowhere to go. Now, I had my own place, a car, and little bit of money in the bank.

Everything seemed to be falling into place, and I knew it was all God's doing. When I needed housing, I found Covenant House. When I needed childcare, the best daycare center in my area just so happened to have one open slot. Usually, infants got put on a waiting list, but I was able to enroll my daughter right away. I found a new job at a health clinic not too far from the daycare, making more money than I had been before. I was surprised to get offered the position after doing poorly in the interview and failing the written test I'd had to take as part of the application process. When I had gone looking for a car, I found a good deal and paid for it in cash. And then, I found the best apartment ever. It was a brand new building, and the best thing was I had a washer and a dryer in my apartment.

It was surreal. I felt like God favored me. I didn't know why, but I was grateful. I never went to bed without praying and talking to God, thanking Him for everything He did for me. That connection I had with Him since I was nine years old was always there. I knew God loved me, and I never stopped going to church. No matter where I lived or who I was staying with, I always found a church nearby. But even with all the tugging and pulling from God, I was being pulled in a different direction.

Chapter 4

From Partying in the Club to Working in the Club

Whenever the weekend came around, it didn't have to be said that I was going out. Just about every Friday or Saturday I was in some nightclub. In my mind, weekends were for partying. I felt like I needed to go out. No matter what I was going through, I forgot about my problems when I partied. Instead of addressing my problems, I danced, partied, and drank them away. At least, that's what I thought I was doing.

Weekdays weren't off limits as I often partied during the week as well, even though I had to get up the next morning for work. The only time I didn't go out was when I couldn't find a babysitter. Partying became more important than spending time with my daughter. There were times when she was with a babysitter for three or four days at a time. At the time I didn't realize how much time I was spending away from her.

Whenever I went out, I wanted to be one of the sexiest girls in the club. Most of the dresses I wore looked like they could have been shirts because of how short they were. I wore shorts that looked like underwear and crop tops to show off my stomach tattoo and my belly button piercing.

I was obsessed with showing off my body. I'd once heard someone say, "If you've got it; flaunt it!" And, that was what I did, and because I posted pictures on social media every time I went out, I felt I had to buy a new outfit every weekend. Sometimes, I ignored household bills just to shop for a new dress or outfit I often wore only one time. Even during the winter, I wore short dresses. Although it was cold outside, it was hot inside the club, and it got even hotter once I started drinking. Sometimes my friends and I drank in the car on the way to the club so we'd already be warm in case the lines were long.

Inside the clubs, it was dark, and the music was blasting, the perfect atmosphere to lose myself and just have fun.   My friends and I had a rule: We would never talk to any of the guys we met at the club. "What happens in the club, stays at the club," we told each other. No matter how fine a man was, dancing with him was as far as we would go—no exchanging numbers and definitely no leaving with him. We knew our outfits were the only reason they wanted to talk to us. Ironically, we didn't want to be bothered with any man who would talk to a woman dressed the way we were.

I broke that rule once. One night, we stood in line outside of the club for over an hour. While standing in line, I started conversing with a guy who was standing behind us. Our conversation continued once the guards let us into the club. The entire night, I only danced with him. My friends teased me calling him my prom date when he and I took pictures together. At the end of the night, we exchanged numbers, and I justified it by pointing out that we met in line, not inside the club.

He turned out to be a very nice guy. I slept with him and continued a sexual relationship with him for a month or so before getting bored. He was too serious, wanting to settle down, and I wasn't ready for that. I just wanted to have fun. I always reminded him where he met me, and that I was not ready to give that lifestyle up.

There were many nights I got so drunk that I didn't remember driving home. I only remembered getting in my car and ending up at home. I got sick a few times, and each time I said I would never drink again, only to find myself drinking the following weekend. My friends and I got a wake-up call when one of our friends left the club alone one night and wrecked her car because she had been driving drunk. She hit a median and ended up on the opposite side of the road. Thankfully, there were no other cars around. She could have killed someone or gotten killed herself. She wrecked her car but only suffered minor injuries. After that happened, we all were more cautious. I still drank but not as much when I knew I had to drive, especially when I had to drop people off.

I kept an overnight bag in my car because I had "friends" I could call on any given night to go visit after leaving the club. "Whose son is going to get it tonight?" I'd say as I scrolled through the contacts in my phone. If one didn't respond, another one would. Sometimes, I'd have them meet me at my house, but on most occasions, I went to them.

If it was a Saturday, I always made sure I left in time to run home and shower so I could make it to church on Sunday morning. As much as I needed to be in the club, I needed to be in church. Most times, the preacher seemed to be talking directly to me. I'd sit in church feeling sorry about the things I was doing and tell myself I was going to stop. But once I went out of those doors, the conviction was gone. Deep down, I wanted to live for God. I knew the things I was doing were wrong, but I couldn't stop. I remember being in church once listening to the preacher and wondering if I was supposed to be ministering to people. I saw myself standing up in a church and speaking to the congregation. I laughed it off. *That could never be me*, I told myself.

Clubs weren't the only place I went for a party. I went into people's homes, and held what were known as passion parties. At these parties, I presented the adult novelty products I sold. The parties were for women, but I sometimes did couple's parties so the men could come too. I hosted parties for many different types of women from stay-at-home moms to lawyers, reporters, doctors, and business owners. I was surprised at how many grown women didn't know simple things about their bodies, things that girls typically learn in middle school, and I found myself doing a lot of teaching. Some people were single and looking for products to satisfy themselves, while others were in relationships or married and looking to spice things up with their mates. I had a website so people could buy online, but doing parties was how I made the most money.

At one point, business was so good I planned to open a physical store. I got as far as looking into buildings, wholesalers, and looking for business grants, but I kept asking myself if the store was something I truly wanted to invest in. I knew I could make a lot of money, but I also knew it wasn't something I wanted to do forever. While I enjoyed it, I never actually felt proud of it. I knew it was a business I would never be able to talk about openly in certain settings, like church. When I told one of my friends this, she laughed and said church people would probably be my best customers. I knew what she meant, but I didn't want a business I had to keep secret, or where people had to buy from me in secret. I continued doing parties and selling from my website, but I dropped my plans of opening a store.

Working in the Club

One day, I decided to become a stripper. I knew men loved strippers, and from what I heard, strippers made a lot of money. I used the excuse that I was only doing it for the money. Although I did need the money, it wasn't the only reason. I had never told anyone, not even my best friend, but I had always wondered what it would be like to be a stripper. I thought they were sexy, and they were lucky to have a bunch of men after them. I wanted to be desired the same way. So, I told my friends I had no choice, and this was something I needed to do. They supported me and told me to just be careful.

I visited a few strip clubs to see which one would be a good fit for me. The first one I went to was downtown, but it was too close to home. *What if my father walked in?* Not that he went to strip clubs, but this club was too close to where he lived. I visited another club right outside of D.C., but there were only two or three girls working at a time, and I didn't want that type of attention. I visited a few different clubs before reaching out to one of my childhood friends who had been a stripper. She told me about a strip club right outside of D.C. I could check out. She said they would probably allow me to start right away, so I needed to be prepared.

I packed a washcloth and soap, some skimpy lingerie, and a bottle of alcohol. I knew I would need plenty to drink, because I was nervous. When I got to the club, I liked how they were set up. *This is it*, I thought. The club manager gave me an application to fill out and asked me to show her my outfits.

"I'll allow you to wear this tonight, but you need to buy some outfits like that," she said pointing to one of the strippers.

"Okay, I didn't know," I told her handing her my application.

She walked me to the dressing room and told me to get dressed and come back out to audition. *Audition?! I don't even know how to dance. How am I going to audition?* I was terrified, but I knew I would be fine once I had a drink.

The dressing room was filled with girls. Some looked very young, barely eighteen years old; some looked to be around my age, while others looked to be over thirty years old. There were many different shapes and sizes, and none of the girls seemed to have a problem being naked in front of the others. Of course, I got stares being the new girl, but a few of them were very friendly and showed me a spot in the corner I could claim. As soon as I sat down, I took out my alcohol and took a couple of shots.

"You gotta hide your drink. It's no drinking or drugs allowed in here," a girl sitting across from me said while pointing to a sign on the wall.

"Thanks." I quickly put my bottle away.

"We all have some, but we keep it in our bags so the guard won't see it."

I nodded.

"What's your name?"

"Kendra."

"No, your stripper name. What do you want people to call you?"

"You gotta think of a name for when they introduce you," another girl interjected.

I hadn't really thought about it. "Just call me Chocolate."

"Okay, Chocolate," the first girl said, smiling.

I got dressed, took a couple more shots of my drink and felt the alcohol began to take its affect. I was ready to audition. I had to pick two songs to dance to, one slow and one fast. I gave them my song choices and went up on the stage. A few of the girls watched as I auditioned. The club had just opened, so a few guys had walked in and were also watching. I have never been a good dancer, but obviously, dancing skills were not what they were interested in. As long as you had a nice body and could shake your behind that was all that mattered.

"Go ahead and get to work," the owner told me. I thanked him and ran back to the dressing room to take another shot of alcohol.

The alcohol had me so relaxed I wasn't even nervous for my first dance. I was just relieved to find out we didn't have to dance on stage. I knew there was no way I could dance on a pole. I had never even touched a pole, and those girls were upside down and twirling all over it. I told myself I was just fine working the floor giving lap dances. Back in the dressing room, I noticed a lot of the girls were using wipes to freshen up. I went to the bathroom several times throughout the night with my washcloth and soap to freshen up.

By the end of the night, I was tired; my legs and feet hurt, and I had only made about $80 after paying my tip-out. The tip-out was the money each stripper had to pay to the club at the end of the night. It was typically a set fee of $20, but if you got caught sitting down for too long or if you arrived late, you had to pay more. I was disappointed, but I told myself I just needed to work harder next time and not sit down as much. On that second night, I made a lot more money. I only sat down when I felt like I absolutely needed to.

~~~

After dancing at the club a few times, I started enjoying myself. At first, I only went some weekends when I felt like making some extra money, but the owner eventually became stricter with the rules. We could no longer just come and go whenever we felt like it. We had to make a schedule and stick to it or find another club. I tried working only two days a week, but we were required to work at least four. Weekends were mandatory for everyone because that was when it was the busiest. I knew the schedule would be too much for me, but I had gotten used to the extra money and didn't want to give it up.

I was now working a full-time job during the day from 8:00 a.m. to 4:00 p.m. I worked at the club two nights during the week from 10:00 p.m. to 4:00 a.m., and Fridays and Saturdays from 10:00 p.m. to 7:00 a.m. Whenever I asked to leave early, I had to pay a higher tip-out. Some nights I just paid it because I was so exhausted. I wondered how some of those girls danced the entire night without getting tired, and then I realized stripping was their full-time job, so they slept all day. I came in from working on my feet all day in a doctor's office.

In addition to the schedule, the owner had also become strict about wanting every girl to go on stage. Some of the girls had complained that they were the only ones going on stage, so the owner made it mandatory that every girl went on stage for at least two songs every night. Besides my audition, I had never been on stage. So when I had to go up, I drank extra. I never did learn how to do tricks on the pole. There were classes on Wednesdays before the club opened, but I never went because I did not want to see that place any earlier than my scheduled shift.

Going on stage meant making more money, but I was okay working the floor extra hard, just as long as I had my drink. I was carefree, and I felt more sexual when I was drunk. A lot of the girls got high, but I preferred to drink. The drinks relaxed me so I could dance. I often closed my eyes and pretended I was dancing for someone I was in love with. It was so much easier to do this with guys I was attracted to.

I was often asked if I ever did more than just dance for money, and by more, they meant sex. I was offended the first time a guy asked, but then I learned that some of the girls did do more than just dance, so they must have figured we all did. One night, this guy I danced for pulled out $500 and told me it was mine if I left with him. I said no thanks and kept dancing. There was no way I was going to risk being raped or killed by this guy. I'm sure he eventually found a girl to leave with him, but I didn't stick around to find out.

I did meet a man who owned a website where men paid to watch women shower. He asked if I was interested, and after thinking about it for a few days, I decided I wanted to do it. *Why not?* I thought. I found his card and gave him a call. We scheduled a day for him to come to my place and film me. I knew he was legit as I had seen his website and knew he was who he said he was, but I had a male friend come over just in case. I felt better with him there. After about thirty minutes of filming, we were done. He gave me my money, and my video was posted on his site that night. It was a paid website, and only subscribers could see the videos, so I didn't worry too much about people I knew finding out about it.

~~~

After a while, I began to wonder if the alcohol was causing me to get tired and hot so quickly. I had to stop and rest often. One night, I decided I wasn't going to drink. I noticed I had much more energy, and I didn't get hot as quickly either. The next night I drank as I usually did, and sure enough I got tired and hot very quickly. So, I cut back on the alcohol, sometimes only drinking at the beginning of the night, but there was something very different about working as a stripper while I was sober. I started to notice things I hadn't noticed before. Some of the guys were calling us names, and I felt disrespected. When I was drinking, I was able to ignore being called the "B" word or a garden tool. But when I was sober, I didn't like it at all. I even felt a hint of shame at one point. When I was drunk, I could be on stage completely naked, but when I was sober, I couldn't bring myself to do it.

Then I started running into people I knew. For months, I hadn't run into anyone and then all of a sudden, I was seeing someone I knew just about every week. I began worrying one of my patients would walk in. I feared running into one of them more than I feared running into anyone else. One night, one of my exes walked in, and my stomach felt like it had dropped to my feet. I panicked and ran back to the dressing room. I contemplated staying in there until he left, but then I thought, *what if he stays all night!* Besides, I would get in trouble for staying in the back too long, so I decided to act cool and approach him before he saw me first.

I walked out and sat in the chair next to him. "Hey," I said, "what are you doing here?"

As I expected, his eyes got big when he saw me. Before he could ask, I told him I was only doing it for the money. He said he understood. We chatted for a few minutes, and then I went back to work. It was awkward when I got called on stage, and I had to dance with him watching. I'm sure if I'd had a drink, his being there wouldn't have bothered me. But, I was trying this sober thing, so I didn't have any alcohol in my bag.

Shortly after that, I ran into a guy from my neighborhood I had known since we were little kids. He actually became my best customer. Sometimes he paid me just to sit and talk with him. I begged him not to tell anyone, and he gave me his word he wouldn't. But of course, he did. More and more people were finding out about my secret.

Working at the club was no longer exciting like it had been at first. I didn't like being disrespected by some of the men. I seldom saw my daughter anymore. I was always tired, so I barely did anything outside of going to work and dancing at the club. The money was no longer worth what came with it. I realized it was time to quit. So one night, I just didn't show up, and I never went back.

Chapter 5

I'm Getting Married! But for All The Wrong Reasons...

Johnathan lived in the apartment building directly across from mine; the first time I saw him, I thought, *Wow*. He was just my type, cute brown skin, long hair which he wore in two strand twists, and he had his own apartment and car. He wasn't like some of the other guys in the neighborhood who sat outside all day smoking and drinking. He kept to himself. I was pretty sure he had a job since we usually got home around the same time in the evenings. He always smiled and said hello when I walked by. I saw him a couple of times as I was leaving out to go to the club and he complimented me but never said anything more. I was pretty sure he liked me, but I wondered why he never asked for my number.

One day as I was walking to my car, I saw him going into his building. I decided I was going to make the first move. I got his attention before he went inside and walked over to him. I introduced myself and told him I wanted to get to know him. I gave him my number, and he called me that night. He said he had wanted to talk to me, but he thought I had a boyfriend. He had to be talking about Antoine. Antoine was someone I saw from time to time, but it was nothing serious. I assured him I was single. We talked a few times that week and went out to eat that following weekend.

The drive to the restaurant was very awkward. We didn't talk nearly as much as we had on the phone. I thought maybe once we were at the restaurant facing each other, the conversation would flow better. It didn't. Before the dinner ended, I already had my mind made up we weren't going any further than this one date. Once we got back home, I was tempted to invite him into my apartment to sleep with him, but decided against it. I gave him a hug and thanked him for taking me out.

After our date, I avoided him. When he called, I was short with him and made excuses whenever he mentioned going out again. We had nothing in common, so I didn't plan on seeing him again. But I couldn't deny the physical attraction. Whenever I saw him, all I thought about was sleeping with him. Eventually, I acted on those thoughts. I invited him over one night and slept with him. After that, my feelings immediately changed. I began reasoning with myself that we were just two different people, and it was okay. *Opposites attract, right?* The fact that we had nothing to talk about no longer mattered. I managed to convince myself he was the man for me, despite feeling no connection to him other than sexual. Besides, it was time for me to settle down with one man. I couldn't keep dealing with different guys.

My friends were telling me not to let this good man get away. He was very sweet and treated my daughter and me well. Plus, he was one of the few guys my age who had himself together. Most were still living at home and barely held a steady job. I was impressed by Johnathan's independence.

Also, I felt secure with him. When I told him I had recently worked as a stripper, he was surprisingly okay with it. He had seemed like the type who would have been turned off by it. I could tell he genuinely cared for me, and I didn't want to let that go.

It took a while for me to fully commit to him, though. Although I'd had boyfriends in the past, this would be my first serious relationship. I made excuses to him saying I wasn't ready, and I needed space. After a few days of not talking to him, however, I'd miss him and ask him to take me back. After going back and forth a few times, I finally committed to a relationship. I was now a one-man woman. I convinced myself and others I was in love.

A few months into our relationship, we began trying to get pregnant. Johnathan's son was nine years old, and my daughter was five years old, so we figured it was the perfect time for us both to have another. After trying for a couple of months, it finally happened. I took a pregnancy test, and it came up positive. To confirm, I took two more tests. Three times I watched as the positive plus sign on the test went from invisible, to faint, to bold. I couldn't believe it. *I was going to have another baby!*

I made a doctor's appointment right away, so I could start my prenatal care. I couldn't wait to find out when the baby would be due. When I got to my appointment, they did another pregnancy test and confirmed it was indeed positive. My doctor estimated I was very early, only about five or six weeks along. They drew blood for various tests and gave me a referral for an ultrasound. I was excited and nervous at the same time. I was excited to be having another baby but nervous about the pregnancy. I hadn't felt any symptoms yet, but I figured they would start at any moment. When I had been pregnant with Kyelia, my symptoms started right away and continued throughout my pregnancy. I hoped this pregnancy wouldn't be the same. I remember thinking, *At least this time I won't be alone.* Johnathan was more excited about my pregnancy than I was, so I knew he would never disappear the way Kyelia's father had.

A few days after my appointment, I got a call from my doctor. *Uh oh,* I thought when I saw her name flashing on my cell phone. *Doctors only call when something is wrong.*

"Ms. Fowler," my doctor said, "your blood levels came back very high. Either you are having twins, or you are farther along in your pregnancy than you think. Once you get the ultrasound, we'll know for sure how far along you are."

She then asked if there was any chance I could be farther along. I told her we had been trying for a few months, but I had been getting my cycle, so I didn't think I was any farther along than what she estimated me to be.

"Well, get the ultrasound. That will tell us for sure," she said before hanging up.

Wow twins! I got even more excited about the thought of having two babies.

The day of my ultrasound appointment couldn't come fast enough. I was getting anxious. I still hadn't experienced any symptoms yet, besides a mild pain in my pelvis. Finally, I could see my baby and put this anxiety to rest. But, when I got the ultrasound, I didn't see my baby. I didn't see anything. The tech took her time trying to locate my baby. She went to get a doctor, and he tried looking as well.

"Well, Ms. Fowler, you are still very early in your pregnancy," he said while looking at the monitor. "Sometimes we are unable to see anything for weeks. I'm going to have you come back in a few weeks, and we'll look again."

Disappointed, Johnathan and I gathered our things and left. I told Johnathan I wasn't going back to that place because those people didn't know what they were doing. I went there to see my baby, and they failed to provide that service. I was about to find out nobody could provide that service.

Since my ultrasound didn't show anything, my doctor decided to keep a close eye on my pregnancy by doing blood work every week. The bloodwork showed how much of the pregnancy hormone, or HCG hormone, was present in my blood. In early pregnancies like mine, HCG levels typically double every week. My levels indicated I was at least eight to ten weeks, surely far enough along for my baby to be big enough to be seen on an ultrasound.

Why were my levels going up if my baby wasn't growing? After researching online, I knew something was wrong. The combination of not having any symptoms, an inconclusive ultrasound, and the pelvic pains all pointed to ectopic pregnancy. Ectopic pregnancy happens when a fertilized egg attaches to the fallopian tube instead of moving down into the uterus. My doctor agreed it was a possibility my pregnancy was ectopic, but it wasn't definite as it hadn't been confirmed by ultrasound.

My next ultrasound appointment wasn't scheduled for another couple of weeks, but I couldn't wait that long. I went to the emergency room because I knew they would do an ultrasound. They found nothing. I went a few days later—still nothing. Both times, I was sent home and told it was "still early."

Johnathan did his best to make sure I was comfortable. He kept a pot of boiling water on the stove for me, as hot compresses were the only thing that soothed the excruciating pain in my right side. When it got so bad that I was balled up on the floor, he took me back to the emergency room. This time I told them I wasn't leaving. I was sure I had an ectopic pregnancy, and they needed to find it. When I went for the ultrasound, the tech said she saw something but wasn't sure what it was. The doctor came in and confirmed that I did, in fact, have an ectopic pregnancy.

It's one thing to have a feeling that something is wrong, but another to have it confirmed. The doctor held me for a few moments while I cried. The look on her face expressed sympathy, but she quickly snapped back into doctor mode and told me my options moving forward. I needed to act quickly as an ectopic pregnancy could be fatal.

If the pregnancy continued, it would eventually rupture my fallopian tube and cause me to bleed to death. I had two options.

I could have the tube surgically removed, which meant I'd be left with only one. Or, I could get an injection that would terminate the pregnancy. Either way, I had a great chance of having another ectopic pregnancy in the future.

After talking over the risks with the doctors, I decided to go with the injection. The thought of having surgery terrified me. I cried as the nurse injected the medication into my backside, not because it hurt, but because I felt like I was killing my baby. I knew I had no choice, but it still hurt.

There was no way a baby could survive in the fallopian tube. I never imagined something like this happening to me.

Shortly after the first one, I had to get another injection because my HCG levels hadn't gone down. A few days later, I found out my levels had more than doubled, indicating my pregnancy was still progressing. I was told I needed surgery right away. In the midst of all the pregnancy chaos, I was moving into a townhome, and I couldn't even enjoy this big moment. Because of the side effects of the shot, I was too weak to do anything.

Everything had been moved into the house and was still in boxes and would remain there until after the surgery. I had never had surgery before, so I didn't know what to expect. I didn't know if I would be sore and stuck in bed for days, or if I would be back to myself right away.

When it came time for my surgery, Johnathan stayed with me while I got prepped. He walked alongside me and held my hand as I was wheeled down to the operating room. He wasn't allowed in the operating room, but he assured me he would be sitting right outside the entire time. I told him to pray for me as they took me to anesthesia. The anesthesiologist was very sweet. She told me exactly what she was going to do. I told her my biggest fear was waking up during surgery.

"No worries," she said. "If you wake up, we'll just knock you over the head, and you'll pass out."

I laughed, and the next thing I knew, I was waking up. A nurse was standing over me calling my name.

"It's over?" I asked, still half sleep.

"Yes." She smiled. "You're in recovery. You'll be free to go home soon."

"That was fast," I remember saying, looking over at Johnathan, who was sitting beside my bed.

"It took about two hours," he said.

"I gotta pee real bad." I tried sitting up but the pain stopped me.

The nurse rushed over to me. "Here, let me help you," she said. "We just need you to use the bathroom, and then you'll be discharged."

Shortly after using the bathroom, I signed my discharge papers. The nurse wheeled me down to the lobby while Johnathan went to get the car. I'll never forget how cold it was that night. All I wanted was my bed.

~~~

Over the next few weeks, I began to feel better with each passing day, but my emotions were all over the place. I was still in disbelief. I was hoping it had been a dream, but the painful scars on my abdomen constantly reminded me I was fully awake. I didn't understand why this had to happen to me. *What did I do that was so wrong? Did I not deserve another baby?* I had all these unanswered questions that were driving me crazy. The excitement I had a month earlier was now gone.

Going to work made me feel even worse, because my coworker was pregnant, and I had to hear her pregnancy stories. She and I had found out about our pregnancies around the same time, and our due dates had been a few weeks apart. I felt bad about not wanting to hear about her pregnancy. It wasn't her fault I'd lost my baby, and I couldn't expect her not to feel excited about hers. I just wished she would be more mindful about flashing her ultrasound pictures around the office. I had ultrasound pictures as well, but mine showed an empty uterus. I faked a smile whenever she told me something about the pregnancy.

Sadly, though, she too lost her pregnancy. She rushed to the hospital one night after experiencing pain and bleeding and found out she'd had a miscarriage. I cried for both of us when I heard the news. She took time off of work for a few days, but the pain in her face when she returned made me forget my own. Immediately I felt guilty. Guilty for not wanting to hear about her excitement. Guilty for resenting her ultrasound pictures. Guilty for wishing she would suppress her excitement for her pregnancy because I was grieving the loss of mine.

I hugged her and held her for as long as I could. We cried together, shared our experiences, and cried some more. I hadn't got as far along in my pregnancy as she had. I hadn't experienced my baby move like she had, nor had I learned my baby's gender as she had. She'd lost her son. For a moment, I forgot all about my own loss and grieved for someone else.

Johnathan had been great during my healing process, running my errands and helping around the house. But, it wasn't long before I began itching for something new again. I missed going out, and I missed seeing other guys. I wasn't used to being with only one person. When I told him I wanted to break up, he tried to talk me out of it, but I didn't want to hear it. There was nothing he could say to change my mind. It was summertime, and I was ready to have fun. And, that's exactly what I did. I partied and slept with a couple different guys, but, after a while, I began missing Johnathan.

Once again, I went back to him apologizing.

And just like that, we were back together.

A couple months after getting back together, we got engaged. I wasn't surprised at all when he proposed. We had been talking about getting married for a while and had already gone shopping for a ring, so I knew it was coming. I just didn't know when. He asked me on Christmas day after we opened gifts.

After the new year, I began planning the wedding. Against the advice of my pastor, we decided it was best for him to move in with me so we could start saving for the wedding. Besides, we stayed together every night anyway. When we weren't at my house, we were at his place, so moving in together made perfect sense.

~~~

For most women, planning a wedding is the most exciting time of their lives. The most exciting thing for me was wearing a wedding dress and walking down the aisle. I don't know if I ever really thought about the marriage that would follow the wedding. I was so focused on the wedding I ignored the mixed feelings I had. I never felt any excitement about becoming Johnathan's wife, nor did I feel entirely sure getting married was what I truly wanted. But, I figured doubt was normal. *Cold feet is what it's called, right?*

We went to premarital counseling twice a month with my pastor, and it was in those counseling sessions I began to realize how different Jonathan and I were. We disagreed on just about everything. When the pastor explained the husband should be the leader of the home, Johnathan asked if it was okay if he did not take that role. He said he felt more comfortable if I was the leader and made all of the decisions.

I had no knowledge of Biblical order at that time, but I was pretty sure I didn't want to be responsible for making *all* of the decisions for my household. In fact, the biggest problem I had with him was that every decision in our relationship was made by me—every outing, every meal we ate, and every movie we watched was all decided by me. Sometimes, I wanted him to suggest a restaurant or plan an activity. Instead, he left everything up to me. Hearing him say that let me know that wasn't going to change after we were married. I wondered if I should be marrying him, but again, I convinced myself I had cold feet. *We can work through this*, I told myself. *We just need to sit down and talk about it.*

In one ear, I had people telling me not to move forward because I had doubts. In the other ear, people were telling me how good of a man he was and I shouldn't let him go.

"Nobody is going to be perfect," they said.

Every time I talked about it with my Aunt Tricia, she would say things like, "Girl, do you know how many women are looking for a man like him? Do not let him go. One day, you're going to regret it."

That stuck with me. Plus, I had been told by a few of my friends that I was too picky, so I figured this was just me being picky again. I continued planning my wedding, but as time went on, I saw more warning signs.

He admitted my past bothered him. He hated that I had been a stripper and couldn't stop thinking about it. This surprised me because in the beginning he had insisted he was okay with everything, but now, suddenly, it bothered him. I was watching an interview on TV, and the woman being interviewed was asked how she knew her marriage was over.

"I knew it was over when we could be in the same house and not speak to each other for days," she said. That sounded like Jonathan and me, and we weren't even married yet. We would go days without talking after having an argument, and it drove me crazy. I realized this wasn't how a relationship should be. We were supposed to be happy and in love. And I never felt like I was in love with him, except when we were intimate. After realizing I didn't want to marry him, I knew I had to tell him, but I couldn't bring myself to do it. I hated the thought of hurting him again. We watched a movie one night that turned out to be the confirmation I needed to call off the wedding. In the movie, the stars played an engaged couple who realized they weren't right for each other and broke up right before the wedding. It was almost scary how similar their story was to my own and how I came across it at that very moment.

Later that night, I told him we needed to hold off on the wedding. I should have completely broken off the relationship, but instead, I suggested a longer engagement. It would be the third time I'd broken up with him, so I needed to be absolutely sure. I didn't want to regret it later.

When I talked to Aunt Tricia about it, she said, "Look, I know what I said before, but it's obvious you are not in love. I don't see you smiling at him, hugging on him, nothing. You can look at people and tell when they are in love, and you are not."

Hearing it from my Aunt Tricia was all I needed. I was finally able to do what I should have done long before, end the relationship for good. This time I was honest and told him I wasn't happy.

"So, you want to break up?" he asked in disbelief.

I nodded.

"You sure?"

"Yes, I'm sorry," I said with my head down. I couldn't look him in his face.

"Okay," he said. "I'll leave as soon as I find a new place."

A couple weeks later as he made arrangements to move out, I found out I was pregnant...again.

Chapter 6

My "Bow Down" Moment

Have you ever had something happen in your life that completely knocks you down? You get so low you have no choice but to call on Jesus? Well, I had this experience, and I call it my "bow down" moment. It's when Christ truly became my Lord.

I had been going to church every Sunday but did not have a personal relationship with Him. Deep down, I desired the relationship, but I just never knew how to begin. I had heard other people testify about knowing the Lord and feeling His presence, but I had yet to have that experience. I could easily tell people about how the Lord kept me alive and how He opened doors, but it wasn't until my "bow down" moment that I could say the Lord comforted me. I used to question whether people who jumped up and down in church were for real or if they only did it for show… Until I broke out in a praise of my own.

~~~

Johnathan and I had officially broken up, but he stayed with me while he looked for a new place to live. One day, as I was standing in line at the dollar store, I saw some pregnancy tests on the counter. I didn't think I was pregnant, but something told me to buy one. I was curious about the accuracy since they were only $1.00. The cashier insisted they were pretty accurate. She said people bought them all the time. *What the heck, it's only a dollar*, I thought.

When I got home and took the test, I was surprised to see a positive result. *Pregnant?! How could I be pregnant? I haven't slept with Johnathan since*…then I remembered it had been a little over a month! I went back to the dollar store and bought two more tests. They both tested positive. Then, I went to the drug store and bought a more expensive test. It also came up positive. I couldn't believe it. I hadn't even thought there was a possibility I could be pregnant. I hadn't even missed my period yet.

Fear suddenly hit me. *What if it's another ectopic pregnancy?* I told Johnathan the news and asked him not to move out, at least not until I got a checkup and knew everything was okay. I didn't mention it to him, but I even wondered if we should go through with the wedding now that I was pregnant.

When I went to see my doctor, she gave me an estimated due date of December 27. *Wow a Christmas baby.* She referred me to have an ultrasound right away since I was considered high risk for another ectopic pregnancy. Knowing this, I detached myself from the pregnancy. I didn't get excited, and I didn't go around telling everyone like I had with my last pregnancy. I only told a few of my closest friends. I decided I would wait until I knew for sure that it was a normal pregnancy.

On the morning of my ultrasound, I was beyond nervous. I couldn't sleep the night before and could barely eat anything. I lay on the exam table as they probed and prodded, looking for some sign of life.

"I'm sorry I don't see anything," the sonographer said. "You are still very early, though."

I instantly broke down in tears. I knew what that meant.

"That's what they told me last year, and it turned out to be ectopic. Ma'am, please look again," I pleaded.

"I don't see anything in your fallopian tube either. Like I said, you're still very early. Don't worry. If we check again in a couple of weeks, we should be able to see something."

I had already heard that too. I got dressed and made another appointment before leaving.

Two weeks later I had another ultrasound, and they still couldn't find anything. Again, the sonographer told me to come back in a couple more weeks. *This can't be happening,* I thought. *God wouldn't let this happen to me again.*

Feelings of relief washed over me as I convinced myself that things like this don't happen to good people twice. I convinced myself I had nothing to worry about, so I let it go…until those familiar pains began in my pelvis. This time the pains were on my left side. I went to the emergency room, and they took me to straight to ultrasound.

When the sonographer told me she didn't see anything, I snapped at her. "Can't you see there's nothing in my uterus? It's got to be ectopic! Please look harder."

I didn't want to go back home without answers. Just as she was about to give up, she said she saw something tiny in my left fallopian tube, but she wasn't certain what it was. At that moment, the nightmare was happening all over again. The inconclusive ultrasounds, the pains, and the sonographer telling me she didn't see anything and then actually seeing something was like déjà vu.

I cried when the doctor came in and confirmed my pregnancy was ectopic. I listened as they listed my options. I initially refused the injection since it hadn't work last time, but the doctor told me there was a greater chance of it being successful this time because I wasn't as far along as I had been with my first pregnancy. I wanted just to have the surgery so all of this could be over, but that would mean losing my fallopian tube and the chance of ever getting pregnant again in the future. Reluctantly, I got the injection. This time it seemed to be working as my HCG levels dropped quickly, but days later the numbers doubled. Again, the injection hadn't work. I needed to have surgery.

I was twenty-six years old and learning I might never again be able to get pregnant. The doctor assured me this was not the end for me. I could get pregnant in the future with in vitro fertilization. I had no time to grieve or feel sorry for myself. My primary concern, at that moment, was doing what was best for my health, and that meant removing my left fallopian tube. They sent me home and scheduled the surgery for two days later.

While at home, all I could think about was the possibility of my tube rupturing. I was afraid to eat, afraid to sleep, afraid to do anything, so I decided I was not going to wait two whole days. I asked my father to keep Kyelia, but he told me to find someone else because he was tired of picking her up. He had picked her up from school a few times while I was going back and forth to the hospital and my doctor appointments, and I guess it was too much for him.

Once I found someone to keep Kyelia, I went back to the hospital's ER the next evening hoping they could do the surgery sooner. I was wrong. I stayed in the ER for hours, waiting to be admitted. When I was finally admitted the next morning, I still had to wait on the surgeon, which was another twelve hours. Throughout the day the nurses popped into my room to check my vitals and to tell me they were still waiting for the surgeon. I had never been so miserable in my life. It had now been over twenty-four hours since I arrived. I was in pain, starving, and all alone. Unlike the first time I went through this, Johnathan was not there with me holding my hand. He would be arriving later to pick me up after the surgery.

It would be an understatement to say I felt relieved when the nurse finally came to take me down to surgery. I never thought I would be excited about having surgery, but I was ready to get it over with. *Here we go again*, I thought as they wheeled me down to the operating room. Both the surgeon and anesthesiologist explained what they were going to do, and what seemed like moments later, a nurse was waking me up.

When I sat up, I was surprised I wasn't as sore as I had been when I had the first surgery. This time, the pain was bearable. I got up with no problem and used the bathroom, and I was discharged a short time later.

One of the nurses wheeled me down to the front lobby while Johnathan brought the car around. *Déjà vu.*

On the way home, we rode in silence until he said, "I'm leaving tomorrow."

I turned to face him. If I wasn't awake before, I certainly was then. "What? You can't leave tomorrow; I just had surgery."

"I'm moving into my sister's house tomorrow," he said. "I'll be getting a U-Haul truck in the morning."

I couldn't believe him. We had agreed he would stay a couple of weeks, or at least until I healed from surgery.

"I just had surgery! How could you leave?" I screamed, hitting him. "You said you were going to stay!"

He had one hand on the steering wheel, and the other hand was blocking me from hitting him. When the car swerved and almost hit another car, I stopped hitting him but continued cursing at him.

When we got home, I pleaded with him to stay a couple more weeks as we had agreed. Although we had broken up, I needed him. I was in pain both physically and emotionally. I didn't want to be alone, but no matter how much I cried, he would not change his mind. He was cold. He even tried to leave that night.

His excuse was, "I can't take seeing you this way."

As he was getting his things together, I followed behind him begging him to stay. Out of anger, I began throwing things at him. I threw everything I could get my hands on. As he walked downstairs, I picked up the vacuum cleaner and threw it down the stairs attempting to hit him with it, but he moved just in time, and it hit the wall instead, creating a big hole. He went out the back door and was about to get in his car but quickly came back inside when he heard a loud boom. I had knocked his flat screen TV off of my television stand and onto the floor.

Just a couple hours after my surgery, I no longer felt any of the physical pain. Instead, I felt anger, hurt, and disbelief. I couldn't believe this man who had loved me so much for the past two years was leaving when I needed him most. I don't know what brought him back into the house. I'm not sure if he came back because he felt sorry for me or if he was worried about me destroying the rest of his things. Whatever the reason, he came back inside, went upstairs, and lay on the bed. I was exhausted, so I lay down beside him and finally fell asleep. For the first time in a while, I was able to sleep.

When I woke up the next morning, he was still sleeping. I looked around my bedroom, and there was broken glass all over the floor. It looked like a tornado had hit my house. I cried as I cleaned up the mess. I felt ashamed. This was the first time I had ever done anything like this. I cleaned up the glass as much as I could and went downstairs. The living room looked just as bad as my bedroom. I attempted to pick up the TV I had knocked down, but it was too heavy. Johnathan woke up shortly after and continued packing. He left and rented a moving truck to move the rest of his things. As he was leaving, I tried one last time to convince him to stay. Even with all my begging and pleading, he still left. I lay in my bed and cried. I couldn't eat or sleep. I was falling into a deep depression.

This went on for a few days until Kyelia came home from staying with my cousin. I couldn't let her see me like that, so I did my best to appear happy. Every day I dropped her off at school and came back home. I wasn't ready to go back to work, so I stayed home all day. Some days, I sat in her class and assisted her teacher. I just needed to stay busy doing something or talking on the phone. It helped me escape my reality and forget what was going on. When I wasn't talking to anyone, I felt depressed and lonely. If I couldn't reach one of my friends, I knew I could reach my aunt. If I couldn't reach my aunt, I could call my best friend. If my best friend was busy, I could always reach my godsister . At least one of them was available to talk whenever I needed to. But one day, not one person answered the phone.

I called my best friend, no answer. I called my godsister, no answer. I called Aunt Tricia, no answer. I called every person I could think of, and not one person answered the phone. I had just dropped Kyelia off at school and was driving back home. As I got closer to home, I began experiencing what felt like an anxiety attack. I couldn't catch my breath; I was sweating, and I had butterflies in my stomach. I sat in my driveway and continued calling, looking for somebody to answer the phone, but nobody did.

I walked into my house and went straight to my room. I had never felt as weak as I did that moment. Everything I had been going through flooded my mind. *I lost my baby, and now I can't have anymore. I'm not even a woman anymore. Why did this happen to me? I wanted my babies. God, how could this happen to me? Haven't I gone through enough? Why do I have to go through this too? This wasn't supposed to happen to me! People are saying, "Be grateful for the one child you already have." I'm thankful, but I can't just forget that I was pregnant and now I'm not. Was it a boy or a girl? Would I have had a son? Or another daughter? Can you just take me, God?*

The pain was unbearable. Johnathan never called once to see if I was okay. My father had turned his back on me. Before that moment, I had never in my life felt like I wanted to die. I pleaded with God to take my life. I just wanted to go to sleep and never wake up. I'd had enough of life, and I didn't want anymore. I fell onto the floor crying, and Kyelia's face popped up in my mind. *She'll be okay without me.* I began thinking about who could take care of her once I was gone.

Wait what is wrong with you? I asked myself. *Leave my baby? And put her through the same pain I experienced when I was ten years old?*

Ever since I became a mother, my greatest fear was my daughter losing her mommy, but there I was, ready to leave her. I was okay with leaving her all alone in the world. I fell to my knees.

"Lord! Please help me; I need you!" I prayed. It was just the Lord and me that day. It was the first time I had ever cried out to God. I poured out everything. I gave it all to Him. Nobody had answered the phone because they weren't supposed to. God had intervened and put me in a position where I had no choice but to fall to my knees and put all my problems at his feet. This was my "bow down" moment. This was the day that my knees bowed and my tongue confessed. Jesus Christ is King of Kings and Lord of Lords.

I had been looking for comfort and peace in everything and everyone, except God. And He made it so I had no choice but to call on Him and only Him. I had been looking for an escape from my reality, but I was brought face to face with my reality that day, and I had two choices. I could either let my reality take me out, or I could face it and begin my healing process. My healing was in Him and no one else. I believe He made it so I couldn't attribute my being okay to anyone but Him. Nobody else was going to get the glory. I was so exhausted from crying and praying I fell asleep for the rest of the day until it was time for me to pick Kyelia up from school.

Things didn't get better overnight, but that day was the

beginning of the newfound reverence I had for the Lord. I began making a conscious effort not to look for comfort in my friends and family that only He could give. I stopped doubting He could help. I started praying again. I testified every chance I got about what He had done for me. I had been at the lowest point of my life, and He showed up because He loves me. I knew I was going to be okay.

After reflecting on everything that had happened, I realized the part I had played in Johnathan leaving. Although he left me at the worst possible time, I couldn't blame him.

I hadn't cared about his feelings so why should he have cared about mine? I was so caught up in my own loss; I never considered how he might have felt. He wanted another child just as much as I did, so he must have been hurt too. And, I hadn't made it any better for him. I was mean, talked down to him, made life uncomfortable for him, and he'd had enough. One day, I reached out to him and apologized for how I treated him, and I wished him the best.

~~~

We can try to plan our lives, but the Lord's plan will prevail (Proverbs 19:21). I had made up my mind I was ready to have another baby because I thought it was a "perfect time." But of course, God had other plans. There were moments when I heard something telling me to stop trying to get pregnant, but I kept trying anyway. And then, I allowed Johnathan to move in with me. My pastor had urged us not to move in together and advised us to refrain from having sex until we were married. He told us things wouldn't go well. Knowing it was wrong, I still did things my own way.

I wasn't happy, but I continued with the relationship even

though I had many chances to end it. There were so many things I could have and should have done differently. Then again, if it weren't for my mistakes, I wouldn't have learned. While everything I experienced was heartbreaking, the good that came from it, was the newfound reverence I had for the Lord.

I wish I could say I gave my life to the Lord and never looked back. That wasn't the case, though. I still had a few more lessons to learn before I truly got it. I had one foot in the church, and the other foot was still in the world.

Chapter 7

Deja Vu

I was finally starting to feel like myself again. A new hairstyle always made me feel better no matter what was going on, so I went to my beautician and got my hair cut into a cute style. I even went shopping for a few new outfits because I had lost so much weight my clothes barely fit. I had been so depressed I couldn't eat anything. When I did eat, it was because I forced myself. I had lost about twenty pounds, and it didn't look good because I had already been skinny. I guess I looked sick, because people often asked if I was okay. One of my cousins bluntly asked if I had been using drugs.

When I told him no, he said, "Well, are you stressed out?"

I couldn't do anything except laugh at him. Only he could get away with questioning me like that. The better I felt, the better my appetite got, and I slowly began to get back to a healthy weight.

Although I was looking better on the outside, I was still dealing with some things on the inside. I had given my life to Christ, but the change didn't happen overnight. I had some issues.

I found myself thinking, *I'm messed up! How come all I want is sex? I hurt good guys but chase after the ones who are no good. Why do I always hurt people I love? Why do I have such a hard time opening up to people? I was affectionate with my daughter, but even with her, I was emotionally distant. I used to be so loving and affectionate, but over the years something had changed.*

I needed to talk to someone I didn't know, so I sought out

a therapist. After a couple of weeks of searching, I finally found one who participated in my insurance plan and who could see me right away. She was located in Silver Spring, Maryland in a small office she shared with her partner, a psychiatrist who specialized in mental illness. At first, I was embarrassed to be there, because I worried about what other people would think. But then I thought, if they were there they must have issues too.

I patiently sat in the lobby waiting for her to call me to the back. I wondered if she would be nice. Would she hold my hand and nod compassionately as I told her my story? Would she interrupt me often? The suspense was killing me. Finally, she opened her door and called my name. She smiled and shook my hand and motioned for me to sit on the couch. I had always wanted to lie on a couch and talk about my problems like I saw on TV. When she asked what brought me in, I didn't know where to start, because I had so many problems. I just began by telling her what had recently happened between Johnathan and me.

I had always heard the two people you want to be completely honest with are your doctor and your lawyer. So, I spilled all the beans from the very beginning. After a couple of visits, she just about knew my entire life story. In telling her everything, I realized I had never truly loved Johnathan. It was all centered on sex. I told her how sex was the center of all my relationships and it determined how I felt about a person. I told her about my sexual behavior as a child and how I learned to bring myself to orgasm. I told her how I often lost interest in a person once we had sex and how I wasn't interested in much outside of sex. She asked if I could remember what triggered the masturbation. I couldn't remember starting; I could only remember doing it as early as the age of three. And I often tried to sit on grown men's laps so I could be close to their penis.

"While it's normal for small children to be curious about each other's bodies at a young age, your behavior was very unusual," she said. "Tell me about your earlier childhood."

I went on to tell her about the physical abuse from my sister, Kelly. I lived with her when I was two to three years old while Mommy was in jail. My sister, twenty years my senior, already had four children of her own at that time. She beat me often and would hold my hands over the fire on her gas stove. This went on until Mommy finally came home and got me.

I didn't tell Mommy about what my sister had done to me until I was about eight years old. She was in shock when I told her because I was so attached to my sister. Whenever she was around, I cried if she walked out of the room and begged her to take me with her when she left to go home. I even followed her into the bathroom and sat on the side of the tub while she took care of her business. Because of that, Mommy found it hard to believe she had abused me.

She said she knew something had gone on though, because when she first came and got me, it took a long time before I stopped cowering whenever Mommy walked toward me. She figured she had been beating me, but she never imagined she would burn my fingers. She confronted my sister, and they got into a huge argument. I remember wishing I hadn't told my mother. It wasn't unusual for them to argue, but this time it was my fault they were.

Besides the physical abuse, I didn't remember anything else traumatic from my early childhood. My therapist asked if I recall ever being touched inappropriately. I nodded yes. I told her about the time when I was sixteen, and my uncle tried to have sex with me. I had to lie and say I was on my period so he would stop trying. When I pulled away from him, he pulled out his penis and began masturbating. While he masturbated, he lifted up my shirt and rubbed my breasts. I stood there disgusted and in disbelief.

When he finished, he cleaned himself off, laughed, and said,

"You so silly, girl. Come on let's go," like nothing happened. At that time I was living with my father. When he dropped me off at home, I should have told, but I didn't. Maybe I would have if I thought my father would have done something about it.

After I had told my therapist that story, I reminded her that my sexual behavior started years before that incident with my uncle. I was pretty sure that had nothing to do with my sexual addiction. Again, she urged me to think back to my childhood. She insisted I had to have been molested and that it had to be the reason why I knew how to orgasm at such a young age.

"Who else lived in the house?" she asked. "Were there men in and out of the house? Could it have been an older cousin?"

I began crying because I couldn't remember. There were a lot of other people in that house. There were babies, big cousins, uncles, and aunts—a real full house. I tried, but I just could not remember. She asked if anyone stood out. I remembered a boy who used to always mess with me. I don't know who he was, and I wouldn't know who he was if I saw him today. He may have been a big cousin; I'm not sure. But, he always made me cry. I remembered him laughing at me whenever I peed on myself. He's really the only one I remember having interactions with.

Could he have touched me? I hated that I couldn't remember. I cried as I thought about my own daughter. *What if some boy had been doing the same to her, and I didn't know about it? Why can't I remember!* Not being able to remember made me angry.

She told me this was something she saw all the time, children subconsciously pushing traumatic experiences to the back of their minds until adulthood when they're forced to face them.

After a few visits with her, I'd had enough. I didn't want to talk about it anymore because I couldn't remember. I decided my time with her was up. She did help me realize though that one of the reasons I was emotionally distant was because I was afraid of getting too close to people and then losing them. I decided I was going to begin working on that.

I went back to work and got back to my routine. I had been working part-time as a medical assisting instructor and working part-time in a doctor's office, and I hadn't been to either job in over a month. I resigned from the doctor's office because the majority of the patients were babies, and I couldn't make it through a day without crying. I left and began teaching full-time.

I also got back to my routine of visiting Aunt Tricia at the nursing home. She had been considerate of what I was going through and had tried not to bother me, but she still needed me. Because of her frequent hospital stays, her doctor had felt it was best she be put in a nursing home until her health improved. But, every time she seemed to be doing well enough to go home, another problem came up, and she would end up back in the hospital. And then, the hospital would send her back to the nursing home. It had been over a year since she had first been admitted into the nursing home. Her bills still needed to be paid, and her house still needed to be cleaned, so I took care of all of that for her. She still hoped she would be able to go back, which is why she refused to give up her apartment.

Once she started dialysis three days a week due to kidney failure, her hope started dwindling. Even if she did go back home, there was no way she would have the energy to leave out three times a week. She had heart failure, causing her to be constantly tired and out of breath, so she never had any strength. She became very depressed at the thought of never being able to go home. She hated the fact that she could no longer get around on her own. She hated she could no longer do for herself what she was once able to do. She hated she had to be cleaned up by someone else every time she made a bowel movement. She often said she was ready to die. I felt sorry for her. Seeing her this way saddened me, but I never let her see me down because I didn't want her to feel any worse than what she already did.

It was on a Thursday morning I saw and talked with Aunt Tricia for the last time. She had been in the hospital for a few days and was waiting for the doctor to discharge her back to the nursing home. I stopped by the hospital on my way to work. When I got to her room, the doctor was there examining her. I noticed she was talking a lot more than usual. I don't think I had ever heard her talk so much. I didn't think much of it, figuring it was the effects of the medication. When the doctor left, she continued talking. I sat and talked with her for a little while and told her I couldn't stay long. When I was getting ready to leave, she asked me to stay a bit longer.

"I have to go to work," I told her. "I'll be back tomorrow."

"Alright," she said, "Take my bag; I don't need it."

"You sure?" I asked her.

She kept everything in that little blue bag—her wallet, candy, her reading glasses, and every other little thing she liked to keep close. I knew if I took it, I would be coming right back because she would need it, so I tried to convince her to keep it. But again, she told me to take it.

"Okay, I'll take it," I agreed, "but if you end up needing it, I won't be back until tomorrow."

She said okay, and I left. If I had known that would be my last time seeing her alive, I never would have left.

The next morning, I woke up to a bunch of missed calls and a voicemail from the hospital telling me to call them right away. I was listed as her daughter and power of attorney so they called me for everything. I figured they were probably calling me to discuss another medication change for her. I called the number and spoke with a nurse.

"Ms. Fowler, your mom took a turn for the worse overnight. We're about to medivac her to another hospital."

I didn't know what that meant, but I got myself together and headed to the hospital they were transporting her to. When I got there, they had yet to arrive, so I waited in the lobby. While waiting, I chatted with an older lady who was there with her son. She and her daughter had been there for a couple of days and were expecting to be there a few more days, so they had packed a suitcase. She had no idea if her son was going to make it.

As we were talking, I saw EMS arrive with Aunt Tricia. I excused myself from the woman and followed them to the room. I still didn't know why she was there, so I was demanding answers. They assured me a doctor would call me in and speak with me as soon as they got her settled into the room.

I went back out to the lobby and chatted a little bit more with the woman I had been talking to. I was relieved when the doctors called me back to the room. *Finally.* The team of doctors told me Aunt Tricia had suffered cerebral hemorrhage (bleeding inside the brain). I listened as they talked, but the severity of her condition didn't hit me until one of the doctors told me I should call any family members who would want to see her one last time.

"Right now she is not breathing on her own. The machine is breathing for her. Even if we take her off the machine, and she breathes on her own, her brain is severely damaged. We can keep her on the machine to prolong her life, or we can take her off to see if she breathes on her own. It's up to you. When we take her off, she may live a couple of days or just a couple minutes. But, I'm afraid there's not much we can do at this point."

Déjà vu. This conversation took me back to the conversation I heard the doctors having with my sister and Aunt Tricia about Mommy when she was on that same machine. And just like my mother, Aunt Tricia had also said she did not want to be kept on life support. So, I knew what I needed to do.

I called as many people as I could think of—family, friends, anyone I thought would want to come to the hospital. Uncle Wayne even came, though he and Aunt Tricia had been divorced for years. A few of my cousins, my best friend, two of my aunts, and I gathered around Aunt Tricia's bed. As I stood there, I thought about how fast this all happened. I watched her stomach rise and fall as the machine breathed for her. I leaned over and lay across her stomach and held onto her so I could feel her breathing.

"Aunt Tricia," I cried. I knew this would be the last time I got to hug her. One of my cousins pulled me up and wrapped his arms around me.

As the nurse began unplugging the machine, I heard her say to Aunt Tricia, "I'm sorry, Ms. Case ."

At that moment I realized I couldn't stay. I couldn't watch Aunt Tricia take her last breath. I ran out the room and into the lobby. Uncle Wayne, the same person who had held me when I was ten years old at my mother's funeral, held me seventeen years later as I was experiencing the pain of losing a mother all over again .

Moments later, everybody came out of the room. Aunt Tricia was gone. We all sat there for a moment and cried. I asked them if she passed right away. One of my cousins told me she glanced quickly around the room before lying back and taking her last breath. I immediately felt guilty. *What if she was looking for me?*

~~~

I began planning Aunt Tricia's funeral right away. She had already told me where she wanted to have her service and where she wanted to be buried. Planning was stressful and seemed never ending. It wasn't until after the funeral that I finally had time to sit down and take everything in. Family and friends who had come into town had gone back home. My phone wasn't ringing as much. Here goes reality again, smacking me in the face.

Aunt Tricia is gone. What am I supposed to do now? I hadn't realized until she was gone my life had pretty much revolved around her—meetings with her doctors and caseworkers, keeping up with her medications, procedures, making sure her bills were paid, and cleaning her apartment. There was always something I needed to do for her. And up until a couple of days before she died, we talked several times a day while I was driving home from work, most nights before I went to sleep, or sometimes we just sat on the phone and didn't say anything.

I felt lost. Some nights, I sat on my couch staring at nothing wondering, *what do I do?* I found myself needing to have a drink every night so I could fall asleep.

~~~

It took a long time for me to be okay after losing Aunt Tricia. I often found myself picking up the phone to call her, and then I would have to remind myself that she was gone. I dreamed about her often, and in several of the dreams, I had to explain to her that she died and each time she asked me what I did with her apartment.

I woke up many mornings in tears. I went through the same emotions as when Mommy died, but this time it was worse. All I could think about was how often Aunt Tricia had spoken about her fear of death, and I imagined her alone and afraid in that hospital room, wondering what was happening as she lost consciousness.

I should have stayed at the hospital longer. Why did I not realize something was wrong? And then, I wasn't there when she took her final breath. The same way I hadn't touched my mother's hand, I had left out the room because I was too afraid of being there when Aunt Tricia took her last breath. It was driving me crazy. It took about a year, maybe longer for the dreams to stop. Even then, they never completely ceased; they only came less frequently.

~~~

I was so unhappy and broken; I jumped from one relationship to another. When things didn't work out with one man, it wasn't long before I was on to the next. I ended up in a very toxic relationship with a man named Bryan.

When I met Bryan, there were so many red flags, but I was so drawn to him sexually, I ignored them all. He didn't have a job, still lived at home, didn't have a car—all those things were deal breakers for me. But I was so blinded by lust I looked past all of those things and past the fact that he didn't have a good relationship with his mother and was disrespectful toward her. I ignored the way he blamed his problems on other people, and that he had children he was barely taking care of.

Over and over I told myself to leave him alone, but it was as if he had some type of hold over me. I'd had guys in the past I'd held onto knowing I should let go, but this was different. It was like I *couldn't* let go. He was very jealous and possessive, which was cute at first because I thought it meant he really cared about me. But after a while, it started to become ridiculous. He accused me of messing with other guys (I wasn't) and flirting with guys in front of him. He went through my text messages and Facebook messages.

We never went one day without arguing because he had a problem with everything. He never admitted it, but I was pretty sure he had a history of hitting women. He never put his hands on me, but sometimes he seemed like he wanted to. He had a lot of anger inside, always yelling and cursing.

One night I called the police because we'd had a huge argument, and he wouldn't leave my house. He was acting crazy, and for the first time, I was afraid of him. When the police showed up, he was very disrespectful, cursing as he gathered his things. I was sure I was done with him that night, but I still could not break away from him because I was addicted to him sexually. A few days after calling the police on him, he was back in my bed.

Around that time, I had started reading the Bible and began to get convicted of certain things. I had already been going to church every Sunday, and I was very involved, but there was never any real conviction until I started reading God's Word.

I had already stopped drinking by that point. One day, I had decided I was going to stop drinking cold turkey. I was out at a bar with one of my friends, and I said, "This is going to be my last drink," and it was.

I wished I could have quit having sex cold turkey, but it wasn't as easy, especially now with Bryan in the picture. I remember thinking, *why did I have to meet him when I'm trying to do right? It's just like the devil to show up when I'm trying to change!* I kept telling myself, *just one more time.* One more time always turned into one more time.

One day, I came across Romans 6:14-15 NLT where Paul says we shouldn't stay in sin just because we have grace. I began to feel bad about taking God's grace for granted. I knew I needed to make a change.

Leaving Bryan was one of the hardest things I ever had to do. So I wouldn't be tempted to let him back into my life, I blocked his phone number, and I blocked him on Facebook. He created fake Facebook accounts to message me, and I blocked those too. He called me from other numbers, and I immediately hung up when I realized it was him. It took a while, but I eventually overcame my addiction to him.

I became passionate about living right, and I wanted other people to do the same. I was like John the Baptist, urging people to turn away from their sins.

Chapter 8

Breaking My Own Heart

Once Bryan was out the picture, I was able to focus on my new walk. I got baptized, stopped wearing revealing clothes, and removed my belly button ring and the ring from my nose. I wasn't just passionate about living right; I wanted to look like it too. People began seeing and acknowledging my change. I went from posting sexual and graphic content on my social media to posting scriptures and inspirational quotes and messages.

I wasn't drinking; I had stopped clubbing, and I had told myself I wouldn't have sex anymore until I was married. I was completely sold out for the Lord. I began studying the Word, listening to and watching different sermons, and reading every book I could get my hands on that would help me on my journey. I was so hungry for the Word, I studied every day.

I called and texted my pastor with so many questions. Almost every week I was talking to him about something I had read in the Bible. I began getting a better understanding of the Word, and asking myself, *do my actions glorify God or do they glorify the enemy?* Pleasing God, glorifying Him, and making Him happy became my ultimate goal.

I set a reminder on my cell phone that popped up every day at 8:00 a.m. "Be pleasing to God today." That's exactly what I set out to do each day. I would imagine God and Satan having a conversation about me like they did about Job in the Bible.

I pictured Satan telling God, "Watch what she does when I throw this her way. I promise she will fall!"

And God would say, "Not my daughter."

I wanted to prove God right every time He said, "Not my daughter." Not that He needed me to prove Him right; He is God, so He is right all by Himself. But, I wanted the enemy to know he didn't have me anymore. There was nothing I loved more than proving Satan wrong! He may have had me for many years, but I was now a new creation in Christ. There was no way he was getting anymore glory out of my life.

At least that's what I thought until I did fall. And I fell *hard*. But it was this situation that was the pivotal point in my life.

I'm glad I fell. Why? Because if I hadn't, I never would have realized how much faith I'd had in myself and my own abilities. I would have never gotten to the root of my issues. I would never have realized the part I played in a lot of the problems I was having. I would never have opened up Proverbs looking for worth and then finding purpose. I never would have started writing this book.

I was so focused on the Lord that I wasn't thinking about dating or sex, and I was doing well. I thought I had this thing all figured out until I met Gerald....

I used to see him at church, and initially I had no interest in him. Not that he wasn't attractive, I had just never paid him any attention. Then he messaged me on Facebook one night and our back and forth messaging soon became a phone conversation. We talked for about three hours that night.

During our conversation, he asked, "So how long have you been celibate?" I was surprised by his question.

"For a few months. How did you know?" I asked.

"I just know," he said. "I watch you and read what you post online. I can tell you are dedicated to God."

I was impressed by how much he had paid attention. It turned out we were both very much into the Word, and we shared a calling to spread the Gospel of Jesus Christ. That conversation turned out to be the first of many. We started off innocently, talking on the phone, going out, and texting throughout the day. We often had game nights at my house with friends.

It was all innocent until we shared a kiss for the first time. Before kissing him, I hadn't thought about him in a sexual way. I was committed to abstinence, and I managed to keep those thoughts out of my mind even when we were alone. But when we kissed, I began to feel something more. I told one of my friends how I felt, and she warned me not to be alone with him again.

"I'm good," I told her. "I can control myself. It was just a kiss."

Again, she warned me: "You're doing good, and I don't want you to slip up."

I assured her I was fine.

Controlling myself became difficult when I started allowing him to stay the night at my house. The first couple of times I managed to resist temptation, but needless to say, I eventually gave in. And when I did, I broke down in tears right in front of him.

It was the first time I had ever felt that much shame. After three months of abstinence, I fell back into sin. I had been doing so well. I asked him to leave my house. He called me the next day apologizing. I told him it wasn't his fault. He hadn't made me do it.

A couple of days later he came over, and we slept together again. But this time, I did not feel shameful. Just like that, I fell right back into what I had fought so hard to be free from. I made excuses to justify my actions. *At least I'm only with one person now,* I told myself as if that made it any better.

We were studying the Word during the day, and sleeping together at night. Things were great in the beginning, but after a while they started changing. He went from trying to win my heart to playing with it. I felt very insecure as he always made me feel like I wasn't good enough for him. One day, I told him we needed to define our relationship, or I was leaving him, but I let him convince me things were fine the way they were. I even fell for it when he made me feel bad about "pressuring him." I knew what it felt like to be pressured, so that was the last thing I wanted to do. So, I went along with it for him. I wasn't happy with the way things were going, but I played it cool so I wouldn't push him away.

I tried to make him see what a good woman I was so he could finally commit to me. I cooked for him, washed his clothes when he came over, and filled out applications for him when he lost his job. I even comforted him when he found out his ex was getting married. It hurt me to see him hurting over his ex, but he said he needed me more than ever. It had been over a year since they had broken up, but it was evident that he was still in love with her. I tried my best to take his mind off of her. I catered to his needs and did things for him I had never done for anyone else, but none of it ever seemed to be enough.

He started drinking heavily and became very disrespectful. His drinking turned me off as he sometimes reminded me of my father when he was drunk. He would talk for hours, "preaching" and not letting me get a word in. I wondered how he could drink so much and then try to preach the Bible. I admit, his knowledge of the Word was what I loved about him more than anything. I thought he would make a great preacher someday.

If only he would stop drinking, I'd think. *If only he'd stop being so disrespectful. If only he'd realize how much I love him. If only he'd commit to me. We would be so happy.*

For almost a year I held on to the hope that things were going to get better. All I kept thinking was that I needed to be a good woman. I didn't want to turn my back on him like other people had. I needed to stand beside him and speak to the great man I knew was inside of him. I was doing so much, trying to prove to him I was a good woman, that I was completely losing myself. I knew I needed to get out of this situation, but I was in love.

One thing I've learned is that when God shows me something is not for me, and I refuse to let it go, He makes it so I have no choice.

~~~

"I'm getting back with my ex," he said, with no regard to my feelings.

I could not believe what I had just heard.

"What!" I screamed at him. I could feel the tears welling up in my eyes, but I refused to let them fall.

He started repeating his sentence. "I'm getting back with…"

Before he could finish his sentence, he hit me on my fist with his face. Okay, so maybe that's not how it went. Maybe my fist reached out and hit his face. Either way, my fist and his face somehow touched. It's not something I'm proud of; I'm actually ashamed to admit I hit him. It had been a couple of years since I had put my hand on someone. I had grown past that. At least I thought I had until that moment.

To say I was hurt would be an understatement. I felt like my whole world had just been crushed. I just knew he was the man I was supposed to be with. Now he was telling me he was getting back with his ex? *How could he "love" me one day and walk away from me the next?*

No one knew what was going on with me except one person I had confided in, because I was too ashamed to tell anyone else. So many people had told me I needed to leave him alone, and the last thing I needed to hear was, "I told you so." So, I grieved in silence.

I felt like I had lost my best friend. For the past year, I had spent just about every free moment with him. We did everything together. When we weren't together, we were talking on the phone. For the first time, I had fallen in love. I loved him more than I had ever loved anyone. I missed him so much, my heart ached. No more sitting on the phone for hours and falling asleep with the phone in my hand. No more weekly Walmart trips. No more sitting in the house on Sunday afternoons watching football. No more hours of watching sermons on YouTube. No more sitting and doing absolutely nothing. I was devastated. I went to sleep with him on my mind and woke up with him on my mind.

I even sent his ex a message on Facebook about how he had called me one night wanting to come over. I didn't let him come, and I'm glad I didn't because it was the last time I had heard from him. I hoped she would read my message, confront him, and leave him. It wasn't fair I was hurting, but he could live happily ever after. I wanted him to hurt like I did. Of course, she did not respond to my message, which made me feel even worse.

I tried everything I could to keep my mind off of him. I read article after article on how to get over a breakup. Some were helpful, and some were useless. One article told me I needed to start dating; it suggested I needed to find a new man, and fast. Another told me our breakup was only temporary and eventually he would come back for me. Holding onto that hope of getting back together was what kept me from healing. Rather than accepting it was over and moving on, I waited for him to call. I waited, and I waited.

Then one day I stumbled upon a blog. I'm sure it was God ordained. The writer, a young woman, had been in a similar situation with her ex. I cried as I read her story, as it was like reading my own. It gave me hope as she eventually let it go and got over it, and I made up my mind that that was exactly what I was going to do.

Gerald wasn't coming back, and even if he did, he did not deserve me. I once read a quote that said, *"If a man can live without you, he should."* I was the prize, not him. Reading that blog was an eye opener. For a long time, I felt like I was lucky to have him, not realizing he was the lucky one. I hadn't looked at myself as a prize.

I realized I had played a major part in my own heartbreak. There had been many warning signs I had chosen to ignore throughout the relationship. Why? Because I was in love, and I thought if I loved him, cooked for him, and met his physical needs he would fall in love with me too. But, it was doing those very things that kept him from committing to me because he didn't have to.

There's an old saying, "Why buy the cow when you can get the milk for free?" I'd heard that saying for years, but I'd never thought about it until it applied to me. One day I researched how much it costs to buy a cow. It costs, on average, $800 to buy an adult dairy cow. Once you buy the cow, you have to make sure it's well fed, healthy, and up to date on vaccinations. You need to clean its bedding and milking supplies . Not to mention, a cow has to be milked once or twice a day. There's a lot of work that goes into caring for a cow. It would be nice to enjoy the milk from the cow and not have to worry about paying, feeding, and caring for it.

The same is true for most men. If he can milk you once or twice a day without having the responsibilities of feeding you, caring for you, and loving you, he will do just that. And, that was exactly what I let Gerald do. He got what he wanted from me without having any responsibilities. He hurt me because I **allowed** him to hurt me.

When Gerald first made it clear he didn't want to be in a committed relationship , I had a choice. I could have walked away, but I chose to stay. And, that meant I accepted his terms. His terms were we could do everything couples do—talk every day, go out on dates, sleep together, and attend family functions. But, our relationship didn't have a title. We were just "friends."

But in the beginning, he was all over me, I kept telling myself. Maybe he was all over me in the beginning, and maybe he did really like me at first. But the moment I gave him my body without requiring commitment on his part, my value went down in his eyes. I've learned that a man can't value a woman who doesn't value herself.

He had no reason to commit to me. I was already giving him all the goods. He wasn't emotionally available anyway, as he was still in love with his ex. I realized this when he found out she was getting married to another man. At one point he sounded like he was crying when he called me and told me. Instead of taking it as a warning sign, I played the supportive non-girlfriend role and told him to take his time and that I was there for him. I tried my best to take his mind off her, but the reality was I couldn't because I wasn't her.

There was nothing I could have done. I was just someone to take his mind off of her for a little while. I should've left him alone and allowed him to sulk on his own. But by this time, I was already in love. I couldn't bring myself to walk away from him, even though I knew I should have. But, he had no problem walking away from me. He'd left without a second thought—no apology, no explanation, and no goodbye. It turned out that she and her new fiancé had broken up and when she reached out to Gerald, he didn't hesitate to take her back.

It was my situation with Gerald that prompted me to start writing again. I had completely lost myself in him. *How did I get here?* I asked myself. *What led to me being so desperate for love that I allowed a man to use and disrespect me? How did I allow him to string me along for almost a year with no commitment? How could I be so stupid as to stay with a man I knew was in love with another woman? I wasn't happy with how things were going, so why didn't I leave him? Why did I allow him to keep hurting me?*

What I soon realized was that I didn't get respect because I didn't command respect. I didn't have to stay with Gerald, and I surely did not have to sleep with him. I chose to. My biggest regret was sleeping with him. I had promised the Lord I would not have sex again until I was married. I had been doing so well, but because I allowed my flesh to control me, I fell. I kept wondering how different things would have been if I had never slept with him.

Would I have stayed around for so long? Or would I have walked away with no problem as soon as he disrespected me the first time? There were so many signs he was not the one for me, but it took him leaving for me to finally let him go.

~~~

So there I was, in pain, broken, and trying to get my fire back for the Lord. I needed that passion I had before meeting Gerald. I prayed for God to reignite my fire. I began praying earnestly and reading His Word, and slowly my passion for Him returned, and it was stronger than before. Inspired by the blog I had read, I started my own. I had completely forgotten about my love of writing until this happened.

Growing up, I had written short stories and poems. I often composed stories about little girls with princess-like lives. I escaped reality and lost myself in my stories. I had expressed myself through poetry. But after I lost all of my stories and poems when my father lost the house, I felt like I lost a major part of me, so I put down my pen. I had forgotten all about my dream of writing books, and my love of writing poetry.

I began writing about love, God's Word, and anything else that was on my mind. I wrote the details of what happened, and what I should have done differently. I became passionate about helping other young women avoid making same mistakes and to recognize when they were breaking their own hearts. So often we blame our broken hearts on men when they were only accepting what we freely gave them.

~~~

We like to blame our crying eyes and sleepless nights
on the MAN who wronged us,
Who told us he loved us,
Who showed no worthiness…Yet, we LET him inside of us.
What if I told you that you were breaking your OWN heart?
And that YOU actually hold all the power right from the start?
But you relinquish it when you agree to do things his way,
Instead of waiting for the real thing
you settle for "ROLE PLAY."
Playing the ROLE of his woman, the ROLE of his wife,
Yet, you are just ONE of the MANY women in his life,
Waiting in line for a TITLE, the chance to be called "his,"
MEANWHILE, you cook for him, clean for him,
and even take in his kids.
I've been there before, so I can relate to the pain,
But I've learned from my mistakes,
and I REFUSE to go back there again.
No need to live in regret because
what's done is already done,

But moving forward you are smarter, much wiser…
now, you are NOT the ONE!
NOT the one he can LAY UP with,
NOT the one he continues to hurt,
NOT the one to be played with…
because now you know your WORTH!
Now, you refuse to settle for less
than what you know you deserve!
Why? Because you've begun studying
the 31st chapter in the
BOOK OF PROVERBS. ♥

~~~

I could easily say I wish I had never met Gerald, but I'm actually thankful for the experience. If it weren't for him, I wouldn't have learned a valuable lesson: people treat you how you treat yourself. If it hadn't happened with him, it would have happened with someone else later. I learned from it, and I vowed it would never happen to me again. And, I meant it.

It forced me to look at my life and examine the pattern I had been following for years. I hurt good men, but I chased after and got hurt by the bad ones. I realized I didn't think I was worthy of being treated right. I had accepted what my father had said about me as my truth. I believed I was exactly what he had said. I was ugly and nasty, and no man could ever truly love me because I was just like my mother.

Deep down, all I wanted was to feel the love and security I'd once felt when Mommy was alive. I had been starving for love since she died, and I looked for it from men, women, anyone who would love me. All my life, I had searched everywhere, except where I should have looked—God.

I went on the amazing journey of getting to know myself. It was then I began the process of overcoming my addictions, healing from my past, and finding my purpose.

Chapter 9

Breaking Free

I remember wondering one day if I had an addiction, but I quickly brushed it off telling myself, *"People with sexual addictions will do it with anyone at any time."*

What I didn't know is sexual addiction does not look the same for everyone. While it may be true that many sex addicts are willing to have sex with just about anyone to satisfy their cravings, it's not true for all. Sexual addiction comes in different forms. Some people are addicted to the act itself, while others are addicted to watching pornography and/or engaging in masturbation.

After doing some research, I found thirty signs and symptoms of sexual addiction, and I had all of them except four. Some of the signs and symptoms included: having sex to cope with life's problems, tying sex to happiness, and inability to focus on things outside of sex.

Having sex to cope with my problems began when I was in high school. The more my father yelled and fussed, the more I wanted to have sex. I always felt like I would feel much better once I had sex. As an adult, I turned to sex when I was stressed out from work. When I was stressed out because of bills, I turned to sex. When I was stressed out because of my daughter's behavior in school, I turned to sex. It was a false sense of stress relief for me. I say false because it wasn't really relief at all. It may have taken my mind off of my problems for the moment, but ultimately it caused more problems. The more I gave in to this addiction, the more power I gave it. The more power I gave it, the less control

I had over my own body. The more I lost control, the more I lost myself.

Because my mind was so preoccupied with sex, I had a hard time focusing on other things. As a child, I looked forward to the next time I would experience that "feeling." I barely made it out of high school because I skipped classes so much for sex. And as an adult, I constantly fantasized about my next encounter. Even seeing certain things at work turned me on and made me anxious for my next encounter. I often rushed my mommy duties in the evenings with my daughter to get her to bed before my "company" came over. I especially had a hard time focusing on things outside of sex while in a relationship.

Sex is what each of my relationships centered on; even when I truly had feelings for the guy I was seeing. I really had no interest in outings, going on dates, or getting to know one another. All I wanted to do was have sex. Gerald was the first guy I genuinely enjoyed spending time with, even if we weren't physical; but even in that relationship, I always hoped our spending time together would lead to sex later that night.

I had a real problem, and once I recognized this problem, I knew I couldn't continue to live like that. I wanted to be married one day, and I knew that would never happen if I continued down the same path. When I was about twenty-five years old, God told me my husband would not be a man I had fornicated with. In other words, my wedding night would be the first time my husband and I made love. Even though it didn't stop me from sleeping around, and it didn't stop me from planning to marry a man I was fornicating with, it was always in the back of my mind. I believed without a doubt God spoke that to me. It *had* to be Him because it surely wasn't something I wanted for myself.

Deep down, I wanted to stop having sex, but I couldn't. Time after time, I told myself, "This will be the last time," and soon after,

I would find myself in someone else's bed. Before I met Gerald, I had gone about three months without sex. At that time, that was the longest I had gone in years, so I figured I had finally gotten strong enough to stop for good. But, I was wrong. A year could have gone by, and I still would have fallen because I had yet to address my problem at the root.

Overcoming

I had enough. I knew I had to do something. I no longer wanted to be a slave to sexual sin. I had been a slave to it my entire life. I had been bound since I was three years old, and I was tired. I was tired of feeling like I couldn't control myself, tired of the shame. I was tired of going through the same cycles. I was tired of hurting people and getting hurt. I was tired of putting my life at risk.

I began praying like never before. I cried out to God, and it was ugly. It was not a pretty cry at all. I had snot coming out of my nose and everything. When you want God to do something for you, you don't care about how you look. It's not even a thought. I just wanted to be **free**. I told Him I wanted to stop and I meant it.

I begged Him, "Lord, please take this desire away!" I asked Him to remove all people and things that would tempt me. "Lord I just want to do better," I told Him. I asked Him to free me of the desire to have sex and masturbate, and to remove same sex attraction.

I prayed this prayer constantly, I fasted, and I read God's Word. Nothing else convicts me like reading the Word. It was scriptures like 1 Corinthians 6:9 and 1 Corinthians 6:18-19 that I read over and over. I can sit under a powerful sermon every Sunday or blast Gospel music into my ears daily, but nothing speaks to me like the living, breathing Word of God. Like the

Psalmist said, I hide God's Word in my heart so I won't sin against Him.

Once I took the time to sit and really think about what I was getting from having sex, I couldn't think of anything. Those few moments of pleasure usually led to regret. For a long time, I was addicted to the "newness" of a person. As strange as it sounds, I was excited about new experiences with new people, and once that experience was over, the excitement was over. And, it would be soon after that I was moving on to the next. The exception to this was when I found a guy I really liked, but most guys won't consider a serious relationship with a girl who so willingly sleeps with them without even going on one date. As much as I tried to convince them, "there's just something different about you," they could smell that lie from miles away. So, I was only fooling myself when I slept with a guy on the first night and expected him to take me seriously.

I also realized I was worth more than sex. While I made many excuses for doing it to fulfill my own desires, I allowed my body to be a playground for multiple men in the process. This is where a lot of us go wrong. We go around screaming, "If a man can do it, we can do it too! Women have needs too!" We love to call it a double standard.

It took me awhile to realize this, but there is a very big difference between a man sleeping around and a woman sleeping around. I am in no way making an excuse for male promiscuity. What I am saying is that a woman's body is not the same as a man's body. This is evident just by looking at both genders. A man's sexual organs are external while the woman's sexual organs are internal.

This may be considered explicit, but let's think about what is happening during sexual intercourse. With each act of sexual intercourse, the woman receives the man. She receives each man, each time. And each time, each man leaves a part of himself within her. So you see, sexual intercourse is not the same for a man and a woman.

In the Old Testament, men could have multiple wives, but women couldn't have multiple husbands. I don't believe this was some rule to imply that women are inferior to men. I believe it was because her body wasn't made to handle multiple husbands.

Let me just insert a praise right here. *Glory!* Women were stoned back in those days for sleeping with multiple men and if that were true today, I would not be here! I'm so glad Jesus came to the scene and said, "Let him who is without sin cast the first stone." *Thank You, Jesus!*

The Woman, God's Most Precious Creation

In Genesis 2:7, God formed Adam out of the dust of the earth. He blew into his nostrils, and he became a living person. But, a few verses later in Genesis 2:21-23, God was a little bit more creative when He made the woman. He put Adam into a deep sleep, took one of his ribs and created His greatest work of art, in my opinion, the woman. Have you ever wondered why He didn't just grab more dust and create the woman as He did the man? I believe He took His time sculpting the body that would be the carrier and deliverer of life. Our bodies are a work of art, custom made.

A woman's body can carry one or more babies at one time, while nurturing and stretching to make room for them! It manages to carry human life for nine whole months, just the right amount of time for a baby to be healthy enough to survive outside of the mother's body. The woman's body is so complex, yet miraculous. Its functions can only be the work of God. Looking at my body the way God sees it changed my entire perspective.

We need to value ourselves more. We need to value our bodies. We need to value the most precious thing in our bodies, our birth canal. It is both an entry and an exit. Two bodies are made into one flesh via entry into the birth canal, and life is brought into the world through the birth canal.

When you see it for how precious it truly it is, you may never allow a man who is not your husband to see or enter into that precious place again.

Sex Is Meant for Marriage

Sex is a holy act created by God for husband and wife to become one, to conceive children, and to express their love toward one another. It was never meant for two unmarried people, although the world leads us to believe we "deserve" this experience. After all, why would we have sexual desires if we're not supposed to act on them right?

Yes, God created us with these desires, but they were only meant to be acted upon within the context of marriage. The world has made sex into as natural an act as eating and drinking. Sex outside of marriage is glorified in TV shows, movies, music, and books. It amazes me how it has even begun to seep into the church. I see many Christians within the church and even leaders attempting to justify sex outside of marriage, saying that it is not clearly prohibited in the Bible.

Let's take a look at what the Bible says about sex before marriage. In the Old Testament, a man could put away his wife and even have her stoned if he found her to be impure—no longer a virgin. If a man had sex with a virgin and did not plan on marrying her, he was charged a fine. While the punishment for women was often far worse than what it was for men, stoning, as I mentioned before, there have always been consequences for sex outside of marriage (Deut. 22:20-29), adultery and also incest.

In the New Testament, Jesus said that whoever looks at a

woman with lust has already sinned in his heart. The thought itself, which precedes the act, is a sin. If the very thought is a sin, surely the act is too.

The Apostle Paul said in 1 Corinthians 7:9 that it's better for the unmarried to marry than to burn with passion. He was referring to those who cannot control themselves. He said this because he knew marriage was the only way they could fulfill their sexual desires without being guilty of sin. If sex outside of marriage was not sin, there would have been no need for Paul to instruct them to get married. Please understand there is no Biblical justification for sex outside of marriage.

Once I was honest with myself, I could admit that sex was meaningless outside of marriage. It wasn't glorifying to God, and most of the time, it left me feeling worse than I had before. I don't think God is being mean in telling us to wait to have sex until marriage. I believe it's His way of protecting us. Sex can create false sense of intimacy. There is a connection that takes place that can make you feel things that aren't really there, and ignore things that are there. There were many times that I held onto men because of the connection I felt during sex that I would not have felt otherwise. There were times I experienced unnecessary heartbreak I could have avoided.

Ladies, take a moment and think about how you felt when things did not work out with a man you never had sex with. Maybe you went out on a couple of dates, and one or both of you realized it wasn't going anywhere, so the relationship ended. No big deal. Now think about how sad you were when things did not work out with a man with whom you shared your body. You felt like a piece of you was gone you could never get back. A piece of you feels like it's missing, because it is. Each time we sleep with a man who is not our husband, we give a piece of ourselves away.

Why do we do this to ourselves? How long will we continue to break our own hearts?

During sex, you become one with the other person. In 1 Corinthians 6:16, Paul explains that when a man has sex with a harlot, he becomes one flesh with her. So not only is he having sex with her, he is coming into covenant with her as if she were his wife. So, if this is true of the man and the harlot, it has to be true of every man and woman who have sex.   Have you ever been so attached to a man that you felt like you couldn't leave him alone? Have you ever been in a relationship you knew wasn't good for you, but for some reason, you could not walk away from it? You couldn't explain why, but you felt he had a hold on you? Have you ever been so attached to someone that, even as they mistreated you, you felt drawn to them?

Maintaining Purity

When I first decided to practice sexual abstinence, I made the mistake of thinking I could sleep in the same bed with a man and not be tempted to have sex. The more I lay in bed with him, the harder it got to resist what my flesh wanted. Eventually, I gave in.

In 1 Corinthians 10:13 Paul told us God will not allow us to be tempted to the point that it's unbearable without providing an escape for us. This scripture makes perfect sense as I look back on the many ways I could have escaped the situations I put myself in.

I once dated a guy who did not have a car so every time he came over, I had to leave my house and get him. I remember one night offering to pay for a cab. There were times when I had to scramble for a babysitter, calling all around town for someone to watch my daughter when I could have just stayed home. I can't think of many situations where there were no obstacles in my way.

I believe those obstacles were my ways of escape, but instead of escaping, I remained in bondage by choice.

I had to stop putting myself into those unbearable situations. Because I knew that lying in bed with a man ultimately led to sex, I promised myself I would no longer allow a man into my bed, nor would I lie in a man's bed.

Initially, it was tough as I was trying to undo a knot that had been tied for years. All it took was one phone call, one text, or even a Facebook message for me to end up right back where I was before. So I utilized the block contact feature on my phone, the unfriend option on Facebook, and the unfollow button on Instagram. By doing this, I cut off easy access. I knew talking to certain people led to certain things.

It is very important to be honest with yourself. If being alone with a man always leads to sex, it's safe to say that you can't be alone with a man without having sex. If kissing a man always leads to sex, it's safe to say that you can't kiss a man without having sex. Being in denial about it only delays the deliverance because you'll never take the necessary steps to be delivered, and those necessary steps include avoiding being alone with a man. We put ourselves into compromising situations to test ourselves. When ultimately, it is not by our own ability we are able to fight the cravings of the flesh, it is by the power of the Holy Spirit within us.

Limiting My Exposure to Triggers

If we're honest with ourselves, reading and watching certain things can arouse us and make us want to have sex. Once I made a choice to be sexually pure, I didn't want anything making it harder than it already was. Even if I didn't have sex, I was tempted to masturbate. For a long time, masturbation was normal to me even when I was too young to realize what I was doing. I never saw it as an addiction until I learned that addiction is any problem or habit that controls a person, and I had been controlled by masturbation since I was three years old.

It was harder to stop masturbating than it was to stop having sex. At first, I made excuses, saying *"at least I'm not having sex,"* but the problem was that it had a stronger hold on me than sex. I would do it and then feel ashamed after. I would do it with the lights off as if I could hide from God. The fact I felt like I needed to hide let me know what I was doing was wrong.

I am in prayer and fasting for that area of my life. I had to modify the playlist on my phone to remove songs that reminded me of sex, and I had to throw away some books. One of my favorite authors as a teen was a well-known writer of erotic books. While it was not those books that caused me to be sexual, they did ignite some feelings I don't think I would have felt if I had never read them.

Those books empowered me to explore my sexuality and not be afraid to act on my desires. There was one book in particular that made me want to be a professional seductress. The way the book glamorized her life made me want to live like her. She came and went as she pleased, slept with whomever she wanted, and nobody dared to speak badly about her. I wanted to be her. In a way, I was her. But, the difference between she and I was that her life was fiction, and my life was real.

I remember at sixteen years old acting out a sexual scene I had seen in a movie. Even as an adult, those steamy scenes made me want to act them out. So, in addition to monitoring what I watch and read, I also unfollowed different pages on social media. I remember one night coming across a post on Instagram, and I instantly was tempted to masturbate. It had been weeks since I had last done it, but that one picture was all it took to fall back into that sin. This is why it's so important to be careful of what we expose ourselves to. Know your triggers and avoid them.

I would be lying if I told you I never think about sex. The difference now is I do not allow it to linger in my thoughts. I counter those thoughts with prayer and pure thoughts as the Bible tells me to do. The more I practice this habit, the easier it gets. When my mind is pure, my actions are pure. While I can't take my virginity back, I am made pure in the Lord. His blood washed away my sins, and now I am a new creation. I am finally free!

Chapter 10

Purpose in My Pain and Healing in My Forgiveness

I had heard the term "calling" a few times, but for a long time I wasn't too sure what it meant. I imagined it to be an audible calling from God that only "chosen people" experience. But then I learned that a calling refers to your God-given purpose, and every single person on earth has one, whether they realize it or not.

Ephesians 2:10 says, "For we are his workmanship, created in Christ Jesus unto good works, which God hath before ordained that we should walk in them."

I began to wonder what my purpose was. I looked around and saw people with incredible talents—singers, actresses, dancers, painters, and cosmetologists. These people had special skills that not everyone has.

But what about me? I cannot sing or dance. I've never been creative. There must be a reason why I was born, I thought.

I began praying, asking God to show me why He created me. "What is my purpose?" I asked him. It began to be slowly revealed to me that I was already walking in my purpose. I was using the gifts He gave me to draw others to Him, so I had discovered my purpose. God had also given me the ability to inspire people with my writing, whether it was a blog post or a poem.

As I shared my testimony with others, I inspired others. It wasn't until I began receiving messages from people letting me know something I had said or written had spoken to their situation that I realized I was onto something. Even people I had once partied with started asking me about this God I often spoke about. It was the best feeling in the world knowing God was using me to draw others to Him, and I became more and more passionate about it.

While listening to one of my favorite Christian radio shows, "Family Life Today," I heard one of the hosts talk about finding purpose this way: "Think about what makes you hit your hand on the table and go: 'I need to do something about that!' Your purpose is almost always connected to something you're passionate about."

That was confirmation for me, because there was nothing I was more passionate about than inspiring others, especially women.

I began to feel a call on my life to minister. I'd experienced many visions of myself ministering to people, but I had brushed them off thinking someone like me could never minister to anyone. *Who would want to listen to me? As many men as I've been with, who would ever take me seriously?? Who do you think you are?* Those were the questions that haunted me. Then one day, I read Acts 9.

In that chapter, Saul was a Christian killing Pharisee who had been transformed into a Gospel preaching, soul-winning apostle. This man who once slaughtered Christians was the same man who wrote the majority of the New Testament. The same man who had declared, "I can do all things through Christ who strengthens me," at one time, wanted to kill anyone who professed Christ.

If he can be transformed, surely I can too, I thought. I began researching the Bible to find other imperfect people God had used, and I learned throughout the Bible He had used what the world would call "messy people." But it is in using "messy people" He is most glorified.

~~~

Lord, Your Word says that in You, I become a new creation,
Which means I'm cleansed of my past,
no more contamination.
Nothing separates me from Your Love,
according to the Apostle Paul,
And this is coming from the same Christian killing Pharisee
formerly known as Saul.
If he can be transformed, surely I can too!
I can go from being used by the enemy to being used by You.
And Rahab, she was known as a harlot,
Was used by You to aid in capturing
the land that was promised.
And Mary of Bethany , even with her past,
Set the example of giving to the Lord your last
By laying at the feet of Jesus and pouring out
the contents of her alabaster flask.
At the feet of Jesus she worshipped,
not caring who was looking and listening,
At the feet of Jesus she repented,
and her sins were forgiven.
Even King David messed up,
and he was a man "after God's own heart,"
But because of greed, selfishness, and lust,
tore one man's family apart.
Attempting to hide his sin, David had him killed.
He had him placed on the front lines of the battlefield.
But even after arranging a murder,
David still had an assignment from the Lord.

It would be through his lineage
that the Messiah would be born!

~~~

My past had bothered me so much because I had yet to make peace with it and heal, and there was no way I could walk in the purpose God had for me while my past held me hostage. It is not God's will for me to walk around in bondage when He has already made me free.

The Bible says in John 8:36, "If the Son sets you free, you are indeed free." He set me free when He bled and died on a cross for me. So why was I keeping myself imprisoned?

Making Peace with My Past

There was nothing I could do about my past. I couldn't go back and change anything, so the only thing I could do was make peace with it. My life depended on it. According to Dr. Harold Bloomfield, author of *Making Peace With Your Past*, our life depends on making peace with our past. And according to a study done by Dr. Vincent Felitti of Southern California Permanente Medical Group, "people who suffered physical, psychological, or emotional abuse as children, or were raised in households marked by violence, substance abuse, mental illness, or criminal behavior, were far more likely to develop serious illnesses as adults—everything from diabetes and bronchitis to cancer and heart disease." Not only did my purpose depend on it, my health depended on it.

Finding the Good

The Bible says in Romans 8:28 that, "All things work together for good to them that love God, to them who are the called according to his purpose." All things include the bad things as well as the good things. So as bad as it was to experience some of the things I had experienced, I can find good in those things. There was a purpose in every bad thing that happened to me.

I went through years of questioning God about the loss of my mother. It wasn't until I began seeing the good in that loss that I was able to heal from it. Experiencing such a significant loss at a young age helped me value life and not take any day for granted. Not to mention, I was raised by the woman who was meant to raise me. My Aunt Tricia played a big part in the woman I grew up to be.

Even though it took a long time for me to get myself together, I never forgot the foundation Aunt Tricia laid for me that started when I was ten years old. She did not pacify me the way Mommy had. Aunt Tricia forced me to grow up while I was living with her. All the years she spent making me do my own laundry, cooking, and cleaning meant I was able to care for my home when I got out on my own.

My love of cooking came from standing in the kitchen with her just about every night. Even up until a few days before she died, she was still coaching me on how to cook certain meals. And, as a child, she didn't give me the freedom to do whatever I wanted to do. If she had, I'm pretty sure I would have ended up in some big trouble. While a lot of my friends did have that freedom and didn't go buck wild, it would have been a different story for me because I was so impressionable. I wanted to fit in so badly I would have done just about anything that everybody else was doing. It was her strict rules that kept me from running the streets.

I was even able to find good in the physical abuse from my sister and the verbal and emotional abuse from my father. I believe it made me extremely sensitive and compassionate toward people. I knew I could never do to anyone else what others had done to me. Growing up, I was always meek and a bit soft-spoken, and for years I saw that as weakness. But when I read, "Blessed are the meek, for they shall inherit the earth" in Matthew 5:5, God told me meekness is simply humility.

Forgiving My Abusers

I once read, "Choosing not to forgive someone is like drinking poison and expecting the other person to die." In other words, we think we're hurting them, but we're only hurting ourselves. That quote changed my thinking. It helped me realize refusing to forgive was not hurting my offenders; it was hurting me.

It was very easy for me to forgive my sister because I've always loved her so much. Ironically, I was very clingy with my sister growing up. I suppose for the same reason a child who is severely beaten by a parent cries to that same parent for comfort after the beating ends. There is an unconditional bond and love there that nothing can stop, not even abuse. So forgiveness toward my sister began at a very early age.

Despite the past, my sister and I had a pretty good relationship. But something changed when I became an adult. I began standing up to her and she didn't like it. She often hung the phone up on me when I disagreed with something she said and then one day she completely stopped talking to me. To this very day, she tells me she does not have a sister. She says doesn't want to have anything to do with my daughter and me. It hurts, but it doesn't make me angry. If she were to call me today wanting a relationship, I would welcome her with open arms.

Most people wonder how I can forgive someone who beat me for no reason, burned me, and tells me she hates me. I would be rich if I got paid every time someone says, "Couldn't be me. If I were you, I would..."

My love for my sister is much stronger than my anger, and it only got stronger when we had a conversation when I was about eighteen years old. She explained why she had treated me the way she had. Her experience with Mommy was much different from my experience. By the time Mommy was sixteen years old, she had already had my sister and my oldest brother. She had another son in her twenties and was thirty-five years old when she had me.

My siblings were in and out of foster homes throughout their childhood because Mommy was a drug addict and alcoholic who ran the streets. My sister told me about some of the bad things that happened to her and my brothers as a result. When Mommy became pregnant with me, my sister was twenty years old and had already had two children of her own and was pregnant with her third.

She admitted she was jealous when she saw how Mommy was taking care of me. She wasn't running the streets as much as she had been when my siblings were children. So when I had to live with my sister, she took all the anger she harbored toward our mother and took it out on me. She felt like it wasn't fair that she had to take care of her baby sister while she had her own children to care for.

This was news to me. It was hard to believe that we had the same mother. I knew Mommy had been a drug addict and alcoholic, but I had no idea my siblings had gone through so much. Although it did not make me feel any differently about my mother, I did wonder how she could have done that to my siblings. I am so grateful I didn't know that side of her. The Mommy I had known was warm, loving, attentive, and funny. I cannot begin to put into words how much love she showed me, so to know my siblings got the complete opposite from her hurt me. I cried when my sister told me what happened to them, and I told her I was sorry they had to go through that. Mommy had never been there for her.

I imagined being a little girl and wanting my mommy to come back for me. It wasn't hard to imagine, because I once was a little girl who cried many nights wanting my mommy. But in my case, my mommy had died and wasn't coming back. In my sister's case, her mommy was alive but had chosen the streets over her. That explained why she was so bitter and, again, it made it much easier for me to forgive my sister. Sometimes, looking at a person's past can help us understand why they are the way they are. While it doesn't excuse the offense, it helps with our process of forgiveness, which is essential for healing.

Forgiving my father was not as easy. While the physical abuse from my sister affected me in some ways, it was the verbal and emotional abuse from my father that affected me well into adulthood. His abuse made me feel like nothing and like I was ugly and unworthy. I blamed my low self-esteem on him. He had pointed out my physical flaws so much I became self-conscious about the way I looked. It was his verbal abuse that made me an angry person. It was the verbal abuse that made me look for words of affirmation from boys and men, because the most important man in my life had insulted me for so long.

It was bad enough I had to deal with the mean things people said to me at school, but I had to come home and hear the same things from my father. I should have been able to run to him for comfort, but I couldn't. I often wondered how he could be so mean to me. *How could he love me and hurt me at the same time?* So, for a very long time, there was a part of me that felt nothing for him.

I hadn't realized I felt like this until I got a call from one of my aunts telling me he had been rushed to the hospital. When she called me, I was at Home Depot. She asked me if I was going to come to the hospital, and I told her I couldn't. It was Sunday evening, and I needed to prepare for my work week. There were a couple more times he went to the hospital, and each time I felt no urgency to rush to his side.

Then it began bothering me my father could be sick, and I felt absolutely nothing. The thought of him dying made me cry, so I knew I loved him. But over the years, I had built an invisible wall that kept me from feeling any affection toward him. I had purposely kept myself from feeling for him because I *wanted* to hate him, but I couldn't. I wanted to be able to never talk to him again, but I couldn't.

I thought I had forgiven my father. I figured I had because I was talking to him, but I realized my reason for communicating with him was the relationship he had with my daughter. He adored her from the first time he laid eyes on her in the delivery room. I have to admit, at first I felt a hint of jealousy because I saw something in his eyes when he looked at her I had never seen when he looked at me—love. That hint of jealously only lasted a moment as it warmed my heart to see his relationship with my daughter. I loved that he loved her so much, and she loved him just as much. So it wasn't that I had forgiven him, I just enjoyed watching him interact with his granddaughter.

I was still holding on to the anger from everything he had ever said and done. I could be having a conversation with him and smell beer on his breath and instantly flashback to those nights he had woken me up just to yell at me. It made me angry every time I thought about it. The fact I still had all of this built up anger toward him proved I had not forgiven him. When I realized I had not forgiven him, I asked God to help me. I wanted to be free from the anger. It wasn't a quick process. It took a few times of thinking I'd forgiven him only to have something happen to make me realize I hadn't.

One important factor in my inability to forgive was I believed everything my father had said about me. Before I could forgive him, I had to realize what he had said about me was a lie. I had to realize I was beautiful, both inside and out. I am fearfully and wonderfully made, which means God took His time uniquely creating me because He loves me. There is no one else like me. I needed to learn to see myself as God sees me, and what He sees is truth.

The only reason my father lied to me was because he believed a lie someone else told him. When I saw my father as the broken man he was, I felt sorry for him. He could only give me what he had himself. Understanding this made it easy to truly forgive him. I didn't keep it to myself. I let him know I forgave him, and I wanted to move forward. I also told him I wanted us to have the father-daughter relationship we'd never had. From then on, things improved. Our relationship got better, and I felt like a huge weight had been lifted off my shoulders.

~~~

Forgiveness is not for our offender, but for us. It doesn't mean we have to allow that person back into our lives to do the same thing again; it just means we are choosing to let go so we can properly heal. It's not about letting that person off the hook, but rather unloosing ourselves, so we're no longer held down. Anger and bitterness weighs us down. Resentment weighs us down. Forgiveness is not always easy, but it's freeing.

When we choose to hold a grudge, we give it power. Take your power back. Choose today to let go of whatever has been weighing you down.

Some people are walking around still holding onto something that happened when they were five years old. For some people, the sound of their offender's voice brings back memories. Sometimes just hearing that person's name causes pain all over again.

This is not how God wants us to live. Forgive that parent who was not there for you, who missed out on the crucial years of your life and all of a sudden wants to show up like nothing ever happened. Forgive that ex who told you they'd never hurt you but did. Forgive the person who robbed you of your innocence. Forgive the murderer who took away your loved one.

I know you want to get back at the person. Nothing makes you happier than the thought of doing to them what was done to your loved one, but it's time for you to let it go. Remember, forgiveness is for **you**, not for them.

Forgiving Myself

One day, I was confiding in a friend about how I cried whenever I thought about how I used to leave my daughter so I could have fun. After listening to me, she asked, "Have you forgiven yourself?" I started to reply, but then realized I didn't know how to answer.

"Well, I've forgiven all of my offenders, including my father."

"I'm not talking about other people," she said. "I'm talking about you. Has Kendra forgiven Kendra?"

I was stuck. I had never been asked if I had forgiven myself.

That conversation made me realize I needed to stop living in the past and forgive myself. It was one thing to forgive my offenders for hurting me, but it was another to forgive myself for potentially harming my daughter. I believe one of the most detrimental mindsets to one's healing is living in regret. It had been a couple of years since I had dropped my daughter off for the weekend so I could party or rushed her to bed so I could have "company," but the regret still haunted me. People often told me

I was great mother, but they had no idea I felt like a horrible mother.

For years, my daughter had acted out in school as a cry for attention, and it wasn't typical behavior. There were many times I had to pick her up because she posed a threat to other students and teachers, from throwing books and chairs to causing her teacher to sprain her ankle. She had met with a psychologist twice a week and had been prescribed ADHD medication. But as soon as I turned my life around, her behavior started to improve.

For years, I kept my cell phone on at work not knowing when I was going to get the call to pick her up. Then, all of a sudden, I wasn't getting any phone calls at all, and it was all because her mommy was finally present. So you see, when I realized how much I had put my baby through, I beat myself up. But, beating myself up solved nothing, and it changed nothing. I constantly reminded myself of what was most important. I had learned from my mistakes, and God gave me another chance to make it right. New day, new chance.

~~~

I walked around in shame…Meanwhile, I'd already been forgiven.
Isn't it crazy how we repent, but then throw ourselves
into a shameful self-pitying prison?
But the Word says whomever the son sets free is free indeed.
This includes the addict, the murderer, and the thief,
This includes you, this includes me.
The devil is a liar, and the truth ain't in him.
He's damned to hell and wants to take all of us with him.
It is a part of his agenda to make us remember who
we used to be, causing us to lower our heads in shame.
To walk around feeling spiritually defeated, emotionally depleted,

mentally weakened like we can never change.
Don't let him fool you like he almost did me,
Had me thinking the Lord couldn't use someone like me.
Our minds and the way we think of ourselves
is how the enemy attacks us first,
But I'm reminded of the 5th chapter of Ephesians at the 11th verse!
Putting on the armor of God, standing firm
against all the schemes of the enemy,
No matter how much he tries, he can't touch the calling that's in me.

~~~

I've realized it is my past that allows me to be able to relate to so many people. I endured multiple forms of abuse and had the same wounds as many others. I suffered multiple losses and mourned like so many others. I overcame addictions so many others are still struggling with. I've been promiscuous, a stripper, and in same-sex relationships. I've been homeless; I've used and been used, and I'm a single mother who makes mistakes. Now, God is using me to help other women who are where I used to be.

Now that I've reconciled with my past, forgiven my offenders, and forgiven myself I am now ready to walk in the purpose God has for my life. It is my mission to glorify God by ministering to teenage girls and young women so they may be healed of pain that cripples them, freed from sins that bind them, and delivered from the need to meet unrealistic expectations set by the world. I want to inspire them through biblical teaching, inspirational writing, motivational speaking, and developmental programs, to think like Virtuous Women.

See ya in the next book!
~Mizz K

About the Author

Kendra Fowler, also known as "Mizz K", was born and raised in Washington, DC. She has one child, a "tween-age" daughter. She has over 12 years of experience in healthcare as a Medical Assistant and is a certified CPR/First Aid Instructor.

She is best known for ministering to others through her writing, blogging, and spoken word.

Passionate about leading others to Christ and inspiring young women, she is very candid when speaking about her past and the events that ultimately led to her transformation.

Visit Kendra online at:

Facebook
https://www.facebook.com/LoveMizzK

Instagram
https://instagram.com/https://www.instagram.com/love_mizzk

Blog
https://lovemizzk.com/

CPSIA information can be obtained
at www.ICGtesting.com
Printed in the USA
BVHW041943300621
610917BV00012B/441